hoe Bay

Herschel I.

MACKENZIE
RIVER

Here is

ALASKA

A N G E

R.

Fort Yukon

ge
airbanks

Tanana River

ALASKA

Scale in Miles

50   0   100   200

V. English

A N G E

C A N A D A

Valdez

HIGHWAY

Whitehorse

Cordova

Mt St Elias

Skagway
Haines

Mendenhall Glacier

Juneau

William
Sound

Douglas

GULF

of

LASKA

ALEXANDER

Sitka

ARCHIPELAGO

Petersburg

Wrangell

Ketchikan

Metlakatla

140°

Annette I.

UTIAN ISLANDS

ISLANDS OF
THE FOUR
MOUNTAINS

Umnak
Nikolski

LANDS

ANDREANOF IS.

Atka I.

MILES 150°

170°

a I. 180°

HERE IS ALASKA

EVELYN STEFANSSON & LINDA C. YAHN

HERE IS ALASKA

Fourth Edition

CHARLES SCRIBNER'S SONS
NEW YORK

ILLUSTRATION ACKNOWLEDGMENTS

Grateful acknowledgment is made for permission to use the following: PHOTOGRAPHS: p. 108, courtesy of Alaska State Division of Tourism; p. 145, courtesy of Anchorage! Convention and Visitors Bureau; pp. 94, 98, 150, courtesy of Alaska Airlines; pp. 160–161, courtesy of Alaska Coastal Airways; pp. xiv, 3, 4, 5, 9, 12, 15, courtesy of Alyeska Pipeline Service Company; pp. 120, 156, courtesy of The American Museum of Natural History; pp. 135, 138, 140–141, by Ted Bank II, courtesy of Monkmeyer Press Photo Service; p. 86, courtesy of Bechtel Corporation; p. 87, courtesy of Bertrand-Marignane; p. 163, courtesy of Alberta Utt Falk; p. 168, courtesy of General Dynamics Corporation; p. 56 (bottom), courtesy of Richard Harrington; pp. 24, 154, by Victor Heusser, courtesy of Geophysical Institute, University of Alaska; p. 130, courtesy of Kodiak Historical Society; pp. 40, 41, courtesy of Dorothe Livingston; p. 51 (bottom), courtesy of Lomen Bros.; title page and pp. xii, 20, 33, 48–49, 53, 55, 57, 59, 62, 64, 67, 69, 88–89, 91, 96–97, 116–117, courtesy of Frederick Machetanz; p. 163, by NARL, courtesy of John Schindler; p. 51 (top), courtesy of The National Museum, Copenhagen; pp. 28, 79, 81, 110, courtesy of Pan American World Airways; pp. 34, 35, 38, 39, 103, 129, courtesy of State of Alaska, Department of Economic Development; pp. 7, 11, 25, 30, 36, 40, 56 (top), 61, 66, 73, 75, 76, 85, 92, 93, 102, 104, 105, 106, 109, 111, 124, 127, 128, 131, 144, 151, 153, 164, 166, 171, by Evelyn Stefansson Nef; pp. 22–23, 82–83, 84, courtesy of Western Electric. MAPS: endpapers, by Van English; p. 17, by Jackie Aher. DRAWING: p. 48, courtesy of Smithsonian Institution.

Library of Congress Cataloging in Publication Data
Stefansson, Evelyn Schwartz Baird, date
Here is Alaska.
Includes index.
Summary: Introduces the unique history and natural beauty of the largest state, focusing as well on recent problems related to the native population, controversial oil and gas pipelines, rapid development, the threatened ecosystem, unprecedented wealth, and the high cost of living.
1. Alaska—Juvenile literature. 2. Indians of North America —Alaska—Juvenile literature. 3. Eskimos—Alaska—Juvenile literature. [1. Alaska. 2. Indians of North America—Alaska. 3. Eskimos—Alaska] I. Yahn, Linda C. II. Title.
F904.3.S75   1983   979.8′05   83-3193
ISBN 0-684-17865-6

1 3 5 7 9 11 13 15 17 19   F/C   20 18 16 14 12 10 8 6 4 2

Printed in the United States of America.

ACKNOWLEDGMENTS

EACH EDITION OF THIS BOOK has had its list of those who shared time and information or provided a connection to persons with special knowledge.

One name spanned the decades: Vilhjalmur Stefansson, husband and mentor for a quarter of a century, whose inspiration provided me with a starting point and continues to influence me today. That same type of confidence was provided for Linda Yahn by her husband, Robert M. Yahn, without which she might never have undertaken the challenge of this fourth edition. Both our thanks go out to him for his time and patience.

Warm thanks and appreciation to:

Former bush pilot Raymond Peterson, President of Northern Consolidated Airlines, who arranged my first trip to Alaska. Through a printer's error he was deprived of proper credit in the first printing of the second edition of *Here Is Alaska*. I hope he is still alive and able to receive this message of my enduring thanks and gratitude.

John Teal, whose untimely death represents the loss of a friend to me as well as to the Arctic.

The Petroleum Institute and, particularly, Keith Hay.

Professor Michael Krauss at the University of Alaska for information about native languages and peoples.

Lael Morgan, whose knowledge of Alaskans was illustrated beautifully in *Alaska's Native People*.

John Bockstoce, curator of ethnology at the New Bedford Whaling Museum, for whaling information.

Nancy Matherly and Margaret Shannon of the Alaska governor's office, Washington, D.C., for their limitless information and enthusiasm.

Don Dickey, Director of Tourism for the state of Alaska.

The offices of Senator Ted Stevens and Senator Frank Murkowski.

Robin Howe for her excellent typing assistance.

Evelyn Stefansson

CONTENTS

Acknowledgments   v

List of Illustrations   viii

Prelude and Thanks   xi

Chapter I   Oil Rush   1

Chapter II   Forty-Ninth State   19

Chapter III   The Natives Come of Age   26

Chapter IV   Fact and Fable   72

Chapter V   Capitals Old and New   101

Chapter VI   Interesting Islands   115

Chapter VII   Other Alaskan Cities   143

Index   173

LIST OF ILLUSTRATIONS

Map of Alaska   endpapers
Farm in Matanuska Valley   title page
"Into the Home Stretch"   xii
Summer on the North Slope   xiv
Aerial View of Valdez   3
Caribou at Prudhoe Bay Oilfield   4
Archeological Survey   5
Prudhoe Bay Oilfield   7
Highway Before and After Seeding   9
Professor Robert B. Weeden   11
Forty-Foot Section of Pipe   12
Alyeska Pipeline   15
Map: Pipeline Routes and Permafrost Boundaries   17
First Newspapers Announcing Statehood   20
The Alaskan Flag   22
Typical DEW Line Station   22–23
Aurora Borealis   24
Cotton Grass   25
Eskimo Family   28
Howard Rock   30
Chief Shake   33
Tlingit Indian Basket   34
Chilkat Indian Blanket   35
Sitka National Monument Park   36
Miniature Totem Pole   38
Ivory Carving   39

Eskimo Women at Point Barrow	40
Whaling at Point Barrow	41
Eskimo Children at Point Barrow	45
Schematic Drawing of an Earth and Wood House	48
Beach of an Old Eskimo Village	48–49
Eskimo Boat Frames	51
Kayakers	51
Paddling Lessons	53
Skin-Covered Umiak	55
"Ski-Doo" and Eskimo Sled	56
Sled Dogs	56
Helping the Dogs	57
Point Hope Eskimo Youth	59
Point Barrow Seamstress	61
Eskimo Mother and Child	62
Rubbing Noses	64
Nunivak Island Children	66
Eskimos on the Back of a Small White Whale	67
Eskimo Boy with Fish-Drying Racks	69
Juneau Ice Fields	73
Small Pontoon Plane	75
Mountains Near Anchorage	76
Horseshoe Lake	79
Stern-Wheeler	81
DEW Line Station	82–83
White Alice Station	84
An Alaskan River	85
Rolligon	86
Hovercraft	87
Indian Fishing Camp	88–89
Petersburg's Harbor	91
Pulp Mill at Ketchikan	92
Juneau Ice Fields	93
Chilkat Indian Dancers	94
Whaling at Point Hope	96–97
Eskimos Eating *Muktuk*	98
Sitka	102
Russian Orthodox Church in Juneau	103

Mount Edgecumbe   104
Sheldon Jackson College   105
Sitka National Monument Park   106
Juneau   108
Juneau   109
Auk Lake   110
Juneau Landscape   111
Village on Little Diomede   116–117
Fur Seals on Pribilof Islands   120
Musk-Ox Mother and Calf   124
Baling Reindeer Skins on Nunivak Island   127
Ugrug or Bearded Seal Mask from Mekoryuk   128
Russian Orthodox Church on Kodiak Island   129
Kodiak's Historical Society and Museum   130
Interior of Kodiak Museum   131
Aleut Housewife   135
An Aleut Wedding   138
Unalaska   140–141
High-Rise Buildings in Anchorage   144
Anchorage   145
University of Alaska   150
Geophysical Institute at the University   151
Automated Laboratory at the Geophysical Institute   153
Radio Telescope at the University   154
Skull from Point Hope   156
Ketchikan   160–161
NARL Laboratory   162
Wolves at the NARL Zoo   163
Max Brewer, First Director of NARL   164
Drum Dance at Barrow   166
U.S.S. Nautilus   168
Shore Lead off Point Barrow   171

PRELUDE AND THANKS

"In my beginning is my end." T.S. Eliot, *Four Quartets*

MORE THAN 40 YEARS AGO, at the beginning of World War II, a handsome, soft-spoken young artist turned up at the Stefansson Polar Library in New York City. He had spent some time at his Uncle Charles Traeger's trading post at Unalakleet, in the center of Alaska's west coast, where he had taken some of the most beautiful northern pictures I had ever seen. His name was Fred Machetanz, he was about to join the navy, and he wanted my husband, Vilhjalmur Stefansson, to write a text for the pictures. Stef said, "I'm too busy with war work, but Evelyn here can do it." Dumbfounded but also newly married, I didn't protest in front of company, but afterward did. "*Of course, you can do it*," Stef said almost impatiently.

Fred had already published. He arranged a meeting with his Scribners editor, Alice Dalgliesh, who invited me to lunch. She became my editor, too, and a good one, for *Here Is Alaska* and the two other books that followed.

Fred has come a long way since those days. In addition to being a writer, film maker, and photographer, he is now Alaska's most famous painter. Known not only from Ketchikan to Point Barrow but in Washington, D.C., and Florida as well, his painstakingly layered oil paintings bring high prices and many honors. He has waiting lists for future work, and his early lithographs have become rare collector's items. Most Alaskans and many in the lower 48 now know and admire his distinctive, luminous northern

xi

"Into the Home Stretch" by Fred Machetanz. The original painting is owned by Senator Ted Stevens and hangs in the Senate Building in Washington, D.C.

landscapes. His varied themes include Eskimos and their winter trail and hunting scenes, sled dogs, polar bears, snowy mountain scenes, and portraits of old sourdoughs and miners.

In preparing the third edition of this book I made another trip to Alaska in 1971. For the first time I visited Fred and his beautiful writer wife, Sara, at High Ridge, their home in the magnificent Matanuska Valley. They entertained with warm, typically Alaskan, hospitality. I took many pictures of them and their guests, who constituted a Who's Who in Alaska. Returning home, I found that disaster had struck. The salesman who had sold me a new camera for the trip had neglected to educate me about a little lever that had to be pushed when indoor flash pictures were taken. All the rolls of film taken at High Ridge, prints of which I had intended to be my thank you to the Machetanzes, came out a beautiful, uniform black!

So it is with some relief and much gratitude that at long last I can say a proper thank you to Fred for a writing career and to both the Machetanzes for friendship, help, and hospitality over four decades. This book is affectionately dedicated to both of them.

I was 29 years old when this book was first published. As this fourth edition goes to press I am 69! Alaska, the world, and I have lived through startling changes in those years. When *Here Is Alaska* was first published I was married to Vilhjalmur Stefansson, the polar explorer, anthropologist, and writer. Following his death in 1962 I married a historian and educator, John Ulric Nef, and to our astonishment we have just celebrated our nineteenth wedding anniversary. At age 60 I went to school, commuting from Washington, D.C., to an institute in New York City for three years to become a psychotherapist. Now I have a new profession and a flourishing practice. Learning something new and difficult "stimulates the phagocytes" as G.B. Shaw says in *The Doctor's Dilemma*. It is my recipe for a happy old age.

Evelyn Stefansson

1 / OIL RUSH

IN 1968 OIL IN GREAT QUANTITY was discovered at Prudhoe Bay on the Arctic shore of the North Slope, and the state of Alaska would never be the same again. The international oil industry arrived in force and irreversible changes took place. In 1969 the state received $900 million in oil and gas revenue, six times the amount budgeted to run the state, enough not only to balance the budget that year but to run the state for the next six years. The promise of future income danced in Alaskan heads, and to many the principal problem seemed to be how to spend so much money. As the good news spread, optimists streamed into the state and the ever-present housing shortage became acute. However, by 1976 the state was again poor, having spent money without regard to the future. It was forced to borrow money from the Prudhoe Bay lease holders by taxing oil reserves but at the same time giving credits against future production taxes. By 1979 oil production reached 1.2 million barrels a day, generating such large payments to the state it was able to repay its creditors and eventually even abolish the state income tax.

Booms were not new in Alaskan history. Gold rushes had peopled the state when it was still an infant territory, but in their wildest dreams Alaskans had not envisioned activity on this grand scale.

Summer on the North Slope dramatically changes the dry, frozen winter prairie into a scene of endless meltwater pools and small lakes. The oil-drilling rigs are conspicuous on the treeless horizon.

Oil has been known to exist in northern North America since the eighteenth century. Indeed, Eskimos had been using oil seeps as an occasional fuel supply for centuries. Katalla, on the Gulf of Alaska, was the site of Alaska's first commercial oil well, and the oil produced from that small field was refined and sold locally for many years. The meaningful history of oil in Alaska, however, began in July 1957 when it was discovered in south central Alaska on Kenai Peninsula in quantities sufficient to exploit profitably. By 1969 five oil and nine natural gas fields were producing, and petroleum had become Alaska's most important cash crop. A pipeline was built to carry gas to nearby Anchorage and refineries constructed to produce the jet, diesel, and heating fuels that previously had to be imported. Plants appeared for producing ammonia and for liquifying natural gas, which was shipped to Tokyo in refrigerated tankers. But the Cook Inlet–Kenai Peninsula oil and gas fields were small compared with the Prudhoe Bay discoveries.

As estimates of the size of the North Slope reserves grew, several oil companies combined and proposed building a hot oil pipeline, 48 inches in diameter, from Prudhoe Bay straight south for 800 miles to Valdez in Prince William Sound. From the deep-water, ice-free port of Valdez, tankers would transport it to the northwest coast of the lower 48 states.

TAPS, the Trans Alaska Pipeline System formed in 1968, was made up of Atlantic Richfield Company (now ARCO), Humble Oil & Refining (now Exxon), and British Petroleum. These companies were joined the following year by Mobil, Phillips, Union Oil of California, Amerada Hess, and Home Oil of Canada, which later dropped out. Two years later this group had developed into the Alyeska Pipeline Service, a nonprofit corporation organized to design, build, and operate the pipeline system. It took its name, Alyeska, from the ancient Aleut word meaning "the Great Land." The same year British Petroleum traded its leases to Standard Oil of Ohio (SOHIO) for 25 percent of their stock but remained a part of Alyeska. The eight oil companies now forming Alyeska were involved in the largest and most

Valdez before the trans-Alaska terminus was built.

expensive project ever undertaken by private industry. The total
cost eventually rose to $8 billion.

The proposed 800-mile Alyeska pipeline was to cover a route 85
percent of which was underlain by the perpetually frozen ground
known as permafrost. It would pass over more than 800 rivers and
streams and cross Alaska's three major east-west mountain chains,
the Brooks Range, the Alaska Range, and the Chugach Mountains.
But before work was begun on the pipeline itself an all-weather
road had to be built from north of Fairbanks to the Arctic Slope.
Except for "Hickel Highway," a road hastily built over the winter

In a Prudhoe Bay oil field, caribou graze unconcernedly in sight of the operating drill rigs.

that was completely useless when the summer thaws came, no usable road existed. An all-weather road was necessary to transport men, materials, and equipment to the northern part of the pipeline project. Since it would cross federal land, permission to build it had to be obtained from the government.

The granting of this permission did not come easily. A second voice began to accompany the deliriously happy oil song of money, jobs, and future prosperity. It was that of the environmentalists reminding that the proposed pipeline and haul road crossed very difficult terrain: mountains, rivers (including the mighty Yukon), permafrost of infinite variety, and earthquake zones. Climatic conditions were also severe. Ecologists began asking embarrassing questions: what would a hot oil pipeline, which the company proposed to bury, do to the surrounding permafrost; what about the fate of the migrating caribou and the Eskimos who depend on them for survival; what would happen to the fisheries if an oil tanker should break apart in a storm? They pointed to the useless Hickel Highway, a deforming scar across

Alaska's beautiful face, and asked about the ecological conse-
quences of this new operation.

In 1969, Walter Hickel resigned as governor of Alaska to
become Richard Nixon's secretary of the interior. His tenure was
short. He was pro-environmentalist, but he was also in favor of the
pipeline. When he and President Nixon publicly disagreed,
Hickel was replaced by Rogers C. B. Morton, who was to play an
important part in preparing the way for the proposed pipeline.

Congress passed the National Environmental Policy Act in
1969, which required an environmental impact statement for all
projects crossing federal lands and evidence that alternatives to
those projects had been reviewed. Combined with environmental
outcries, native suits disputing ownership of the land virtually
shut down progress on the road.

*Archeologists surveyed the entire route of the 800-mile Alyeska pipeline
before it was completed.*

An alternative to the pipeline was tried in the summer of 1969. One of the Prudhoe Bay oil companies sent its 1,005-foot-long tanker *Manhattan*, the largest ship ever to penetrate Arctic waters, on a much-publicized Northwest Passage voyage designed to test the feasibility of bringing oil directly from the North Slope by ship. It began its 10,000-mile round trip journey on the Delaware River near Philadelphia. Despite heroic and glowing bulletins issued regularly during the course of the voyage, it was found to be impractical. The *Manhattan* reached Prudhoe Bay and Point Barrow, but several times it was caught fast in the pack ice and freed only with the help of U.S. and Canadian icebreakers. The tanker was damaged but managed to return safely and even tried again in 1970 with similar results.

Although the *Manhattan* project failed and the pipeline has long been completed, research and planning still continue in search of better ways to transport oil by ship through these icy regions. On February 11, 1981, the icebreaker *Polar Sea*, in an effort to test whether year-round sea traffic was possible in this region, arrived off Point Barrow, becoming the first American ship to sail that far north in the winter. Thick ice forced the ship to cancel its plans to continue on to Prudhoe Bay, which lies 200 miles east of Point Barrow. The 399-foot ship had punched its way through ice up to four feet thick. Later that year, in March, the *New York Times* reported that the biggest names in Japanese shipbuilding were joining forces to build a revolutionary supertanker to carry oil from the Arctic Ocean. This heavy-duty icebreaking tanker would be longer, deeper, and narrower than conventional oil carriers and would be double-bottomed and double-hulled to minimize danger from an oil spill. An oil spill in the Arctic would be a greater than usual ecological disaster, because in frigid temperatures the oil decomposes very slowly and would remain on the ocean surface for years.

Another alternative to the pipeline that was considered was the proposal made by the Canadian government in March 1971 that an oil pipeline following the Mackenzie River route to Edmonton be substituted for the trans-Alaska pipeline. The Canadians said

The oil field at Prudhoe Bay is a noisy place while drilling is in progress. The automated recorder registered a depth of 7,414.5 feet when this picture was taken.

it would be cheaper and safer from an environmental point of view.

Noting that the 2,600-mile Mackenzie Valley route, although longer than the Alyeska route, crossed no earthquake zones and required no transhipment by oil tanker, some ecologically-minded opponents of the Alaska route agreed. They believed that all North Slope oil should be brought south through Canada's Northwest Territories and Prairie Provinces, using the same river valley route as the planned Canadian gas pipeline. This would bring oil directly to midwestern United States from where it could be distributed more efficiently. The Friends of the Earth, the Wilderness Society, and the Environmental Defense Fund joined forces and filed suit for a permanent injunction against the building of the Alaska pipeline. They claimed insufficient consideration had been given the Canadian route.

Other environmentalists opposed the Canadian route for

different reasons. It was almost three times as long as the proposed route; therefore it would disturb that much more territory. More important, a pipeline that crossed the North Slope into Canada would disturb the Arctic National Wildlife Range. Even if the pipeline skirted the range it would stimulate further searching for new sources of oil in the area. Then Secretary of the Interior Rogers C.B. Morton, in defending the Alyeska route, decided that for national security reasons the pipeline should be on U.S. soil and exclusively for U.S. use. He also pointed out that gas and oil cannot be transported through the same pipeline or even share the same route. Oil is hot, 160° F, when it emerges from depths of 8,000 to 9,000 feet at Prudhoe Bay, and may even increase in temperature as it flows through pipe. Gas can be cooled until liquid and transported at below freezing temperatures. A gas pipeline can therefore be buried in the permafrost without damaging it, while a hot oil pipeline must be elevated to prevent deformation of the permafrost. The pipeline company that earlier proposed to bury the pipeline, after studying the difficulties, came to the conclusion that about half of the 800-mile line would have to be built above ground because of permafrost.

Permafrost varies in thickness from a few inches to the 1,330 feet found south of Barrow. It is composed of frozen earth, ice, rock, or gravel, or any combination of those materials. Between the top of the permafrost and the vegetation cover above it is an area known as the *active layer*, which unlike the permafrost thaws and freezes with the seasons. Scientists usually divide permafrost into three zones: *continuous permafrost*, where all the ground below the active layer is always frozen; *discontinuous permafrost*, where some ground is and some isn't frozen; and *sporadic permafrost*, ground that contains islands of frozen earth. Vegetation that grows above permafrost acts as a kind of heavy quilt that prevents the action of the sun from penetrating downward. After more than a half century of permafrost engineering research we know that the best method of coping with it is to *keep it frozen*, whether one is building a road, airfield, pipeline, or log cabin.

In permafrost land the turning wheels of a heavy vehicle will

LEFT: *A highway after construction in June 1970.*
RIGHT: *In August of the same year after special seeding and fertilizing.*
This grass will hold the soil until natural vegetation takes over.

kill the fragile vegetation it crosses. When the vegetation dies and
turns brown it begins to absorb the heat of the sun's rays instead of
deflecting them as living vegetation does. The absorbed heat
thaws the surrounding earth, which becomes a muddy and
unstable area that slowly and continuously enlarges, like a giant
oozing wound. Trees growing in permafrost areas have shallow
roots that grow out horizontally in the narrow active layer. When
a chain saw cuts a path into such a forested area, the sun thaws the
path, releasing the previously frozen roots. The wind soon topples
these trees the way hail levels a field of ripe grain. Once the
blanket cover of impermeable vegetation is disturbed, the
deformation of the exposed landscape is certain unless measures
are taken to forestall the inexorable process. Among the many

studies made by the oil companies was one to test various types of fast-growing grass seeds to determine which was best to plant in areas disturbed by their activities. In fact, hundreds of types of grasses from all over the world were tested until they came up with four different mixes that they could use at different points on the pipeline route. Planting time had to be considered carefully also, because the growing seasons would be different at different points on the route. The results were a successful planting scheme that would aid in erosion control until nature could take over once again.

Alyeska was involved in considering many matters that had to be decided upon before the actual construction of the pipeline began. One of these was the kind of pipe to be used on the pipeline. It was known that pipe that would be welded and installed in Arctic Alaska had to have special low temperature characteristics. This meant using steel with a low carbon content. The pipe had to be unusually ductile so that it could change shape slightly in extreme temperatures without being damaged.

Alyeska had established that 48-inch-wide pipe would be used in building the pipeline, but by the late 1960s there had not been any long-length 48-inch pipe manufactured. Inquiries about the type of pipe Alyeska needed were sent to steel companies in Japan, England, Germany, and Italy, as well as to nine companies in the United States. The companies were also told that the 800 miles of pipe had to arrive in Alaska by the fall of 1969 in order for Alyeska to keep to its construction schedule. When bids were actually submitted no American companies could meet either the specifications for the pipe or the delivery schedule. Therefore, in April 1969 a joint contract for $100 million worth of pipe was given to Sumitomo Metal Industries, Nippon Kokan Kabushiki Kaisha, and Yawata Iron and Steel Company. Although at that time it seemed like a great deal of money, by the time the pipeline was completed nearly eight years later, it would prove to be a remarkable bargain.

The pipe was delivered in 40- to 60-foot sections, which were wrapped in a protective coating, and they were welded into 80-

Professor Robert B. Weeden of the University of Alaska's Department of Wildlife and Fisheries poses in the 48-inch-diameter pipeline "for scale."

foot "double joints." These were then stored at Valdez and Fairbanks until they could be transported to the pipeline route. Storage time was longer than Alyeska had expected because of delays caused by the lawsuits that had been filed and problems related to getting the necessary federal permits.

A series of events cleared the way for pipeline construction. On December 18, 1971, President Richard Nixon signed into law the Alaska Natives Claims Settlement Act (see p. 27 for details), removing a formidable barrier to the building of the pipeline. When the U.S. purchased Alaska from Russia in 1867 we agreed to respect the rights of the aborigines. There had been much talk but little action in this area until oil industry pressure resulted in the relatively speedy settlement of the long-standing land claims of Alaska natives, also lifting the land freeze resulting from those claims and from environmentalists' lawsuits, allowing the pipeline to overcome its first and biggest obstacle.

A 40-foot section of pipe for the pipeline is guided into the Fairbanks pipeyard.

Meanwhile, the U.S. Department of the Interior considered the wisdom of issuing a permit for construction of the pipeline. Three years and three months after receiving the pipeline proposal, on May 11, 1972, Secretary of the Interior Morton gave his official approval. Before doing so he and his department produced one of the most massive reports (even for a government department) in history.

The 1973 "energy crisis" took place just as pipeline legislation was being considered in Congress. It may have been just the spur needed to speed up the legislative process and clear the way for the pipeline construction. In October the same year, when the Arab members of the Organization of Petroleum Exporting Countries instituted an oil embargo limiting the amount of foreign oil entering the States, pipeline legislation became a burning issue.

On November 16 President Nixon signed into law the Trans-Alaska Pipeline Authorization Act. It granted Alyeska permission to build the pipeline, much of which would be crossing federal land. In return Alyeska agreed to meet certain requirements. An Affirmative Action program would be set up for minority hiring. Always a requirement of government projects, this was the first time a privately financed operation was required by law to do so. Alyeska also agreed to hire natives to fill some of the jobs on the pipeline even if it meant recruiting and training them. Alyeska complied by hiring 5,500 natives and offering $220 million in contract bidding opportunities to native and other minority companies. The act provided for government surveillance of compliance, with Alyeska paying the costs. Still another requirement was the setting up of an oil-spill liability fund to pay for cleaning up any spills that occurred on land or at sea.

The act included a much debated amendment proposed by Alaska's Senator Mike Gravel that was approved by the Senate only after a tie-breaking vote cast by Vice-President Spiro Agnew. The amendment limited further judicial review of the project and stated that permits granted under the law for both pipeline and haul road could not be challenged by the National Environmental Protection Agency (NEPA). Opponents felt it wrong to exempt the pipeline from NEPA's review, but Alyeska had, in fact, already met *all* NEPA's provisions.

The final obstacle was overcome on January 23, 1974, when Interior Secretary Morton issued Alyeska the long awaited right-of-way permit. Construction of the haul road was begun at the end of April, and when it was completed 154 days later it became Alaska's first permanent secondary highway north of the Yukon, as well as the first American highway to cross the Arctic Circle. It is made of highly compacted gravel and graded according to very strict specifications. Three hundred sixty miles long, it includes the first bridge to span the great Yukon River.

As the haul road was completed, Alyeska realigned itself as a company with the corporation shares divided as follows: SOHIO, 33.34 percent; ARCO, 21 percent; Exxon, 20 percent; British

Petroleum, 15.84 percent; Mobil, 5 percent; Union Oil, 1.66 percent; Phillips Petroleum, 1.66 percent; and Amerada Hess, 1.5 percent.

Now work on the pipeline proper began. The first pipe was installed in the Tonsina River in March 1975 and the last nearly two years later. About 420 miles of the pipe were buried and the remaining 380 miles elevated on supports or pilings. There are six pumping stations along the route, and the line has 151 control valves. The nerves and the brain of the system are a computer control center located at Valdez. Alyeska had cause to celebrate when the first oil left Prudhoe Bay on June 20, 1977, arriving at the Valdez terminal eight days later. The S.S. ARCO *Juneau* was the first tanker to be loaded, and it left port on August 1.

Alaskan opinion had been far from unanimous regarding oil development. It ranged from those who saw in the oil business salvation for the state and the solution of all its problems, to the other extreme, those who viewed it as the gravest threat to the last pristine U.S. wilderness, not one acre of which should be despoiled. The environmentalists, many of them Alaskans who wished oil had never been discovered in their state, had pledged their efforts to prevent Alaska's exploitation. Time has educated both sides, and now, with the pipeline completed, it seems clear that it is possible to both develop and conserve at the same time.

The environmentalists must be credited with educating the public and the oil companies. The oil companies must be credited with a new commitment to cherish and preserve the environment. They hired numerous ecologists and scientists to integrate pipeline construction with conservation. The scientists taught them how to proceed in Arctic and tundra Alaska with minimum damage to the environment. At great cost, careful consideration was made of the dangers of disturbing permafrost, vegetation, wildlife, river beds, and archeological sites. They studied the enormous amount of literature, instituted many new studies at the University of Alaska and elsewhere, and took the necessary precautions at every step of oil and gas development from searching, drilling, and production, to building and maintaining a pipeline and tanker shipments.

An important dividend of oil exploration in Alaska was the discovery of some 20 natural gas fields, usually but not always found in conjunction with oil. Drilling has reached below a depth of 13,500 feet in the Cook Inlet–Kenai Peninsula area. Here both onshore and offshore gas fields are supplying fuel to Anchorage and also producing the 47.5 billion cubic feet per year that are cooled, liquified, and shipped to Japan by tanker. Alaskan gas is relatively pure, 99 percent methane, with very low air-polluting sulphur content. With the North Slope oil discovery, gas was found also. The Alaska Natural Gas Transportation System (ANGTS), the name of the proposed gas pipeline company, seems to be running into some of the same opposition faced by

More than half of the 800-mile Alyeska pipeline is built above ground, set on vertical support members buried deep into the permafrost. Heat fins atop the supports dissipate heat from the ground and maintain the permafrost condition.

Alyeska. At $8 billion the oil pipeline price seems cheap compared with the estimated cost of $40 billion for this gas pipeline, which would begin on Alaska's North Slope and cross the mountains and arctic sections of Canada south to California and east to Illinois. In 1977 President Jimmy Carter approved the pipeline project, stipulating that it was to be privately financed without government funding, and that consumers could not be charged for construction costs until the system was finished. Controversy has delayed the start and now has been stirred up again as Congress passed, in 1981, a waiver package with a pre-billing provision that allows the pipeline's sponsors to charge consumers the full cost of building each segment of the line as it is completed.

Meanwhile an Alaska state committee headed by former governor Walter J. Hickel proposed a new plan for utilizing Prudhoe Bay's 26 trillion cubic feet of gas. They presented it on January 17, 1983, the day Japanese Prime Minister Yasuhiro Nakasone arrived in Washington, D.C., to discuss ways of reducing trade tensions between the two nations. The Hickel group proposed a Trans-Alaska pipeline, 820 miles long, from Prudhoe Bay to the Kenai Peninsula where the gas would then be liquified and shipped to Japan. This much shorter pipeline (almost 4,000 miles less than ANGTS) would cost $25.5 billion, compared with the $43 billion projected cost of ANGTS. The Trans-Alaska plan would reduce the U.S. trade deficit with Japan and strengthen our relations with that nation. Alaskans would gain from taxes imposed on the pipeline and from a 12.5 percent royalty on the gas. They favor the plan and forsee a future Japanese gas market where they could command a higher price than in the U.S., where the natural gas market is glutted. ANGTS is currently held up because of financing problems, and its projected completion date of 1986 is still uncertain.

During World War II the U.S. Army Corps of Engineers built the first oil pipeline entirely above ground from the Canadian Norman Wells oil fields to Skagway, Watson Lake, and Fairbanks. It was the first large-scale project of its kind and introduced thousands of workers to the North Country's muskeg, tundra, and permafrost. Sixteen hundred miles of pipe were laid over the

most difficult kind of northern terrain without disaster. The pipe
was of far smaller diameter than the 48-inch Alyeska line—only
four and six inches in diameter. When the war and emergency
were over, the Canol (Canadian Oil) project was dismantled.

Oil and gas discoveries in Alaska have changed her economy
considerably and will continue to do so. In 1981 Alaska was
realizing $4 billion a year in royalties and taxes from oil

*Map shows the Alyeska oil pipeline, as well as the formerly proposed
route along the Mackenzie River. Pictured on the inset are the proposed
routes of the ANGTS and Trans-Alaska gas pipelines.*

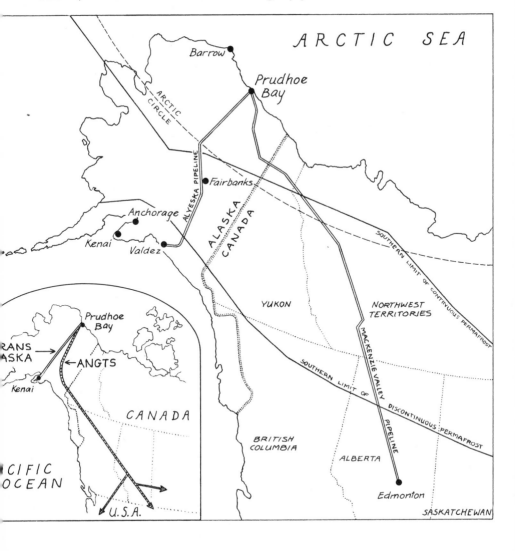

production, which provided 89 percent of the total state revenue. The "problem" of what to do with all this money has Alaskans divided. Some want to spend it without regard to the future. Others worry about what will happen as oil production at Prudhoe Bay tapers off, probably within the next five years. Among projects the state legislature is presently considering are the building of a refinery at Valdez, a satellite system for two-way communication between isolated towns and urban areas, and the Susitna Dam. Former governor Jay Hammond had other ideas. He proposed putting the money in a permanent fund and paying out regular checks to residents that would be reduced when legislation needing funding was passed. He felt that in this way citizens would take more interest in how these resources are spent. The Permanent Fund, the name given the oil income pool, was established by popular vote in 1976. One quarter of oil royalty income goes into this fund. In Governor Hammond's last year in office, the state distributed $1,000 dividend checks from the fund to each Alaskan. Newly elected governor Bill Sheffield disagrees with these dividend payments, especially in view of falling oil revenues. New leadership will provide new solutions to how Alaska deals with these and other problems that arise as an estimated 9.4 billion barrels of oil and 26.5 trillion cubic feet of gas reserves are developed.

II / FORTY-NINTH STATE

O
N THE NIGHT OF JUNE 30, 1958, the U.S. Senate, by a vote of 64 to 20, touched off a gigantic celebration that extended from Alaska's mild, wooded, southeastern shore to its northernmost permafrosted tip, Point Barrow. Huge bonfires had been prepared, and the moment word was received they were kindled by jubilant crowds. Bands, speeches, fireworks, parades, shouting, and dancing in the streets were all part of joyous demonstrations that lasted through the night and well into the day. For the bill the Senate had passed at 8:02 P.M. assured the admission of the Territory of Alaska into the Union as our forty-ninth state. On August 26, in the heaviest election turnout in Alaska's history, her people voted five to one in favor of statehood.

Alaska was ready for this moment! Three years before she had adopted the Tennessee Plan, a program drawn up and first applied in 1796 by the vigorous pioneers of the Territory of Tennessee in *their* fight for statehood. The first item called for by the plan was a constitutional convention. In September 1955, therefore, Alaska's Territorial Legislature elected 55 convention delegates, and the following November they gathered on the campus of the University of Alaska to draft a constitution.

Continuing according to the Tennessee Plan, the convention provided for the immediate election of two "senators" and a "representative" for Alaska to go to Washington. These phantom

19

The first newspapers announcing statehood.

legislators, who had no legal status in Congress, were charged with going to the capitol to lobby for Alaskan statehood. Former Governor Ernest Gruening was one senator-elect, and William A. Egan, of Valdez, president of the constitutional convention, the other. (Egan later became the first elected governor of the new state of Alaska.) Ralph J. Rivers was the lone representative. Combining forces with Alaska's beloved congressional delegate, E.L. Bartlett, these well-informed, able men brought to the attention of Washington and the nation reasons why Alaska should become a state. In the time between his governorship and his "senatorship," Gruening had written a penetrating political history of the Territory, called *The State of Alaska*, setting forth past misgovernment, present problems, and the arguments favoring statehood. Young Mike Stepovich, the first Alaska-born governor, had also helped the fight; so too had the secretary of the interior, Fred Seaton, the first man in his position to interest himself deeply in Alaska and her problems.

To the majority of Alaskans, alerted and tense, word of statehood arriving by radio and telephone brought news of victory—a battle won. Statehood meant an end of colonialism and "taxation without representation." In the past, while Delegate Bartlett might make speeches in the halls of Congress, he had no vote, despite the payment of federal income taxes by his constituents. Statehood meant at last the possibility of controlling the largely absentee-owned fishing and mining industries. Almost since the purchase of Alaska in 1867, these industries had drained her riches. Money, equipment, even labor, came from outside and profits went outside, leaving Alaska depleted in natural and financial resources. But perhaps the most important reaction to statehood for Alaskans was a happy feeling of equality with all other U.S. citizens—a coming of age.

The Alaska Statehood Act permitted the selection and setting aside of more than a fourth of Alaska's total area—103.5 million acres—as state land. It excepted from this land any territories claimed historically by native Eskimos, Indians, and Aleuts. The remainder was assigned to the federal government, and some of it was set aside for parks and monuments.

A portion of the rich dowry Alaska brought to her union with the United States was her strategic position. On the north Alaska faces the Arctic Sea, newest aerial and submarine crossroads of the world; to the west across the Bering Sea and Strait lies the Soviet Union. Two huge, costly defense alarm systems were built to guard these shores. One, the DEW Line, or Distant Early Warning radar screen, was created in 1952. The second is White Alice, a complicated communications system using huge twin antennas, that provided certain communication between outposts and mainland in an area where radio blackouts occur at unexpected intervals and may last a fortnight. White Alice, the latest in tropospheric electronics when it was completed in the mid-1950s, was completely taken over by RCA, a private corporation, in 1976.

Since 1930 Alaska's population has been growing steadily. In 1982 Anchorage and its environs had 173,017 people, and Fairbanks and suburbs had grown to 51,500. They are now booming cities, complete with tall buildings, modern housing developments, motels, parking meters, and traffic problems. The state's rich resources are being developed, some of them for the first time. Fishing and mining, long the most important industries, now have competition from the defense industry, pulp manu-

ABOVE: *Alaska's flag, "eight stars of gold on a field of blue" forming the Big Dipper and the great North Star, was designed by a 13-year-old Indian boy. Benny Benson, a seventh-grade pupil at the Mission Territorial School at Seward, won first prize in the Alaska Flag Contest. His simple, handsome design was officially adopted by the Territorial Legislature in 1927.*

RIGHT: *From the air, a typical DEW Line station's cluster of buildings and equipment surrounding the dome-shaped housing of the main search antenna.*

facturing, and, most recently, petroleum and tourism. In 1973, ten times the number of tourists, over 200,000 of them, visited Alaska than had done so two decades before, and this number rose to 660,000 in 1981. Don Dickey, director of the state's Division of Tourism, says that the projected figure for pleasure travelers for 1985 is one million. Tourism is probably the industry of the future for Alaska.

Alaska is our largest state, two and a quarter times the size of Texas. Her area, 586,400 square miles, increased the total square mileage of the United States to more than 3.5 million. Her islands and indented shores added more than 33,000 miles to U.S. coastlines. Her soils and mountains contain numerous deposits of natural gas, fabulously rich oil lands, and possibilities of almost infinite hydroelectric power. Alaska contains 17 of the 20 highest peaks in the U.S., as well as 20,320-foot Mount McKinley, the

The aurora borealis paints Alaska's skies with light and brilliant color.

Long summer days produce a rich cover of grasses, flowers, and shrubs.

highest mountain in North America. Residents of Alaska, with a per capita personal income of $14,190 in 1981, made more money that year than residents of any other state. Alaska is our only state extending into the Eastern Hemisphere, for the Aleutian Islands reach beyond the 180th meridian to about 170° east longitude. This is a big, tall, wide, rich, record-breaking state!

Though she lacks numbers, Alaska's population is younger and more energetic than that of other states. The average Alaskan is four years younger than the average citizen in the rest of the United States. This youthfulness may be responsible for the fact that although it has the lowest death rate of any state, it also has the highest accidental death rate. In 1980 her population numbered 400,481, up a third from 1970, of which 64,047 were Eskimos, Aleuts, and Indians.

Alaska has grown and changed in many ways since becoming a state in 1958. Some things remain the same—the large areas of startlingly beautiful untouched wilderness, the uncertain weather and extreme temperatures, and outside the cities that open, friendly frontier spirit. Perhaps the single problem that is debated more often and with the most emotion is what might be called "the problems of the rich"—how to handle the recent accumulating wealth from Prudhoe Bay oil royalties and taxes. How and where these monies are spent may determine Alaska's destiny.

III / THE NATIVES COME OF AGE

THE SAD OLD STORY of primitive man's first encounters with so-called civilized man was acted out in Alaska just as in other states and parts of the world, except that it happened more recently in Alaska. Friendly, curious, and trusting, until taught differently, Alaskan natives were easy prey for the Russians, who killed many and virtually enslaved others in the interest of the fur trade. After the purchase it was our turn, and we decimated the native population too, albeit unintentionally, through the biological warfare of measles, whooping cough, and tuberculosis. This was followed by an equally disastrous kind of sociological warfare resulting in native poverty, malnutrition, and, more recently, loss of self-esteem, alcoholism, and suicide.

At first the natives were the dominant people and white invaders a minority, usually in need of something—food, clothing, furs, information, or transportation. It is one of history's ironies that these roles are now reversed. Today the white man and his ways prevail and the natives are the minority. Although the natives number 64,047 according to the 1980 census, an increase of more than 10,000 over 1970's figure, they now account for only 16 percent of the state's population. The white man is rich and the native is poor. The white man is healthy and the native is sick with the white man's diseases. The white man is educated but the natives have been badly, sometimes cruelly, taught, and, until recently, always in a foreign language, English.

Crowded into poor villages and urban slums, deprived of their former hunting grounds by state, federal, and big business land takeovers, they suffer from what is fashionably called "culture shock," a phrase that gives little idea of their miserable lot. Necessity has forced their dependence on white man's food, fuel, and shelter, all of which cost money. But there are few or no jobs in the little villages, so a native must leave his family for a larger village or a city. There he seeks a job to earn the money to buy the goods the white man has taught him—indeed, forced him—to need. Coupled with Alaska's notorious high cost of living (for a family of four in Anchorage it is 28 percent higher than the national average for an urban family), it is small wonder that Alaskan natives are troubled, frustrated, and even hostile. Professor George Rogers of the University of Alaska coined an unforgettable phrase of profound insight that sums up the lot of Alaska's natives when he wrote that they live in "a fragmented ghetto," a ghetto located in numerous small villages throughout a vast territory.

As U.S. citizens Alaskan natives are entitled by law to schooling (indeed the law insists on it), certain welfare and health services, social security, and other familiar benefits. In reality, spread out over an immense and often harsh territory, those farthest from the city administrative centers sometimes receive a fraction of their due and sometimes none at all.

At long last a turn has been made on this grim road. It is marked by the Alaska Native Claims Settlement Act, which was passed by Congress and signed into law by President Nixon on December 18, 1971. One hundred and four years after the purchase, the land claims of Alaska's original inhabitants have finally been appropriately recognized—not to everyone's delight, to be sure, but on the whole a better, fairer arrangement than many had hoped for.

The new law has affected the lives of all Eskimos, Indians, and Aleuts in the state, as well as those residing elsewhere. It enabled them to select and own 40 million acres of designated land and called for $962.5 million in federal appropriations and mineral royalties from oil production to be paid them. This has been accomplished through the formation of 200 village corporations and 12 larger regional corporations in which every native has been able to participate. A thirteenth corporation was established for those natives living outside the state. The act defines a native as any U.S. citizen of one-quarter or more Alaskan Indian, Eskimo, or Aleut blood or combination thereof. The natives were listed with the Bureau of Indian Affairs in one of the largest projects of its kind ever attempted by the United States.

Ten years later, since most of the corporations established by the settlement act have yet to declare a dividend, practically none of the billion dollars received by them in the settlement has filtered down to individual natives. The corporations have, however, created many paying jobs for natives in urban areas, though hunger is still prevalent in remote villages when hunting is

An Eskimo family.

poor. Under the terms of the act the natives, as stockholders, are a captive audience, since until 1991 shares in these corporations are transferable only by death and divorce settlements.

The emergence of native political and financial power has created major changes in villages and towns. The old distant Bureau of Indian Affairs boarding schools, which forced pupils to be separated from their families, are being phased out, and local high schools are now being built. As a result of new sanitation systems, clinics, native health aids, and improved radio and satellite communication between the most remote villages and hospitals in urban areas, native health statistics are at last on a par with those of white Alaskans. Transportation is improving. Few villages in the state are without at least a small airstrip, and the southeastern villages have gained easy access to the outside world through the Alaska State Ferry System.

Subsistence hunting and fishing were essential to more than 70 percent of natives at settlement. Transition to a cash economy has occurred but not easily or completely. Communities with fewer than 200 people account for 20 percent of all Alaskan natives, and nearly 50 percent live in villages of 200 to 300. These small communities offer few jobs, and welfare payments often cannot make up the difference between local food gathering and needed purchased goods. As communities grow, supplies of the fresh game necessary for health often become scarce.

For the natives, new ways of thinking are required; the very idea of *owning* land was strange, for instance, to a primitive Eskimo. The idea of Indians cooperating with traditional enemies —the Eskimo—might seem impossible to an old-timer but is becoming reality. The circumstances that finally brought about the land settlement made the old modes of operation obsolete. One element in the success was a new understanding of how to operate in a white man's world. Where the natives lacked technical knowledge—say, in the law—they hired lawyers and called in experts and advisers to guide them. Thus they were able to accomplish in a decade what they had previously been unable to do in a century.

Howard Rock, the influential and universally admired Eskimo founder of the Tundra Times.

One important part of the activity leading up to the settlement was the establishment in 1966 of the Alaska Federation of Natives (AFN), which was organized specifically for the purpose of obtaining a land settlement. It recently celebrated its fifteenth anniversary with a celebration in Anchorage. During the 1960s 24 separate native groups were formed, from the northernmost Eskimos to the southernmost Indians and including the western-most Aleuts. Despite differences and rivalries, ancient and modern, for the first time in history these people were consolidated into one authoritative voice speaking for all the natives of Alaska.

Before the AFN could come into being, groundwork had to be laid. The American Association of Indian Affairs began to operate in Alaska and helped organize two pioneering events: the establishment in 1961 of Inupiat Paitot (People's Heritage), the first native Eskimo organization; and the birth in 1962 of the *Tundra Times*, the first Alaskan newspaper dedicated to native problems. Howard Rock, an Eskimo, directed the former and edited the latter. He became a respected, influential writer and spokesman for the native point of view. In dedicating *Alaska's Native People* to Rock, author Lael Morgan described him as a man "who sacrificed a promising career as an artist to edit the *Tundra Times* for the Eskimo, Indian, Aleut Publishing Company, because he really believed in Alaska's native people and their remarkable way of life." Rock died in 1976.

Aleuts, the smallest native group, numbered approximately 16,000 in 1741 when Captain Vitus Bering's Russian ship landed in Alaska. At that time almost every habitable island of the Aleutian chain was occupied and some had many villages—Unalaska, for instance, had 24. Aleut numbers decreased through Russian massacres, and they were relocated by the Russians for better control and more effective use in hunting. Some were taken as serfs to hunt seals in the previously unoccupied Pribilof Islands, 200 miles to the north. After the purchase, Americans continued to treat the Aleuts as serfs for another century. This slavelike existence was enforced by federal policies that substituted food and clothing for cash wages and that restricted travel, and also refused to permit unwanted outsiders to enter Aleut villages. When, in 1964, a candidate for the Alaska legislature was barred from campaigning on St. Paul's Island, U.S. Senator E. L. Bartlett of Alaska took up the cause of federal dominance of Aleuts on Pribilof Islands. His bill, the Fur Seal Act of 1966, gave Aleuts local government powers. Then, in 1978, ownership of the island passed to the Aleuts' village corporation under provisions of the settlement act.

The Aleuts were coastal people using the interior of their islands for gathering stone materials, berries, greens, and roots. All else was obtained from the ocean and its beaches. Ancient dwellings were large, communal, partially underground structures built of logs, posts, and sod. Occupants entered through holes in the roof, using notched logs as descending stairs. Interiors were separated with mats and heated by stone lamps filled with oil. Similar, but smaller, structures called *barabaras* were used after the Russian occupation.

Of all western Alaskan people, Aleuts were the most concerned with funeral rites. Important people were placed in boxes with personal belongings after being embalmed. Aleuts did not fear the dead nor did they have ceremonial houses.

Long known for their fine crafts, Aleuts wove baskets, mats, and clothes from the grass that grows so abundantly on their islands. Atka Island women are particularly skilled in the fine art of basket making.

Today, the natives of the Aleutian Islands are a diminishing race but maintain a hopeful outlook. The settlement act gave them a means of gathering together with an economic base, enabling them to develop the rich resources of their region.

The second largest group of natives is the Indians. They can be divided into two general groups: the Tlingit and Haidas, coastal people who lived on the heavily wooded archipelago and mainland of southeastern Alaska; and the Athabascans, who dwelled in the interior.

Athabascans, the largest single group of Indians in North America, include their cousins in the lower 48, the Apache and Navajos. Alaskan Athabascans were divided into seven separate groups: Ahtna (Ahtena), Eyak, Ingalik (Tena), Koyukon, Kutchin, Tanaina, and Tanana. Only the Tanaina and the now almost extinct Eyak lived on salt water. Tanaina lived on the shores of Cook Inlet and the Eyak moved down the Copper River to the delta, settling at Cordova. Vast Athabascan lands contained a spruce and birch growth called *taiga*, as well as large rivers. Fish from these rivers did not provide a sufficient food supply, however, and the seminomadic Athabascan were kept on the move in a constant search for game, principally caribou, moose, and rabbits. The coastal Tanaina were able to build permanent villages, often for more than 100 people. Like the Aleuts, they built barabaras for their homes.

Eskimo and Indian rivalry was often fierce and bloody. However, Ingaliks traded and socially interacted with Eskimos. Except for the Ingalik, who through this interaction adopted the Eskimo wood-carving and painting skills, Athabascans were noted for their lack of interest in art. They did, however, tailor

Chief Shake was a famous leader of the Tlingit Indians.

clothing from caribou and moose hides, some of which they decorated with quills and scraps of fur.

Alaska's panhandle has been home to the Tlingit, Haidas, and Tsimshians. The prosperous Tsimshians, who live mostly at Metlakatla, and the Haidas, whose fathers migrated from British Columbia about 400 or 500 years ago, are small segments of large tribes still living in Canada. In the old days the Tlingit Indians, who live in the southeastern part of Alaska, had a wealthy, aristocratic society that included slavery, a considerable unwritten literature, and the *potlatch*.

The potlatch was a public celebration where, to the accompaniment of singing, dancing, dramatic recitations, and feasting, a man would give away highly valued gifts. Here a new totem pole would be dedicated, marriages celebrated, claims and proclamations announced, and fine clothes displayed. At first glance, it would seem to be a scheme for pauperization, for a chief might give away most of his possessions, including huge dugout canoes and prized Chilkat blankets. But a careful tally was kept of all presents, and rigid etiquette demanded that all gifts be returned with interest, which might run as high as 100 percent. In effect, the potlatch was a banking system and a form of insurance, invest-

A Tlingit Indian basket made of spruce root.

Chilkat Indians, part of the Tlingit family, are famous for their valuable blankets, which predate so-called modern art.

At Sitka National Monument Park some of Alaska's finest totem poles have been preserved.

ment, social security, and credit circulation. If a gift-giver died, the return gift was owed to his heirs. To avoid payment was unthinkable. Traditionally, all gifts were supposed to be of the finest workmanship, made from the best materials. So the potlatch raised the quality of every form of art, whether in weaving of mats, baskets, and blankets, or the carving of jewelry, gift boxes, canoes, or totem poles.

Totem poles, usually placed at the entrance to a man's house, commemorated a special event or, through animal symbols, the family totem, or family tree. Many of the surviving poles in Alaska have been preserved, carefully restored, or reproduced. Fine examples may be seen at Sitka National Monument Park, at Saxman Park outside Ketchikan, at the Juneau Museum, and elsewhere. These great works of native art, once ignored and permitted to decay, are now widely appreciated. During the tourist season, they are among the most photographed items in the land.

Unlike the Eskimo and Athabascans, the Tlingits, as well as the Haidas, had a rigid class system and were concerned with the acquisition of wealth. This wealth was made possible by an abundance of salmon, halibut, and herring, which was the main food for both Indian groups. Slaves, who were usually war captives, were another sign of wealth in their culture.

Currency was not used; instead, the blanket was a basic unit of exchange. The Chilkats, a northern Tlingit group, wove the famed Chilkat blankets. Hereditary lineage crests were often used as designs. Originally, blankets were clothing worn with a buckskin skirt for women and a breechcloth for men. The comparatively mild climate of the Tlingit lands sometimes permitted nudity and going barefoot.

Today, social and economic status is visible when the Sealaska Corporation meets annually in Sitka. Sealaska, which is number 951 on *Fortune* magazine's list of 1,000 largest U.S. companies, is one of the 13 corporations established by the Native Claims Settlement Act. It is owned by 15,800 Indians all from the southeastern region of Alaska. The company's directors are all

There is a renewal of interest in native crafts in Alaska. It includes the restoration and preservation of old totem poles and the making of new ones, some of them miniatures that will be sold as souvenirs.

Indians, but they have relied on the experience of others by having white men as managers. 1980 earnings of $5.9 million were largely from timber sales and the operation of Ocean Beauty Seafoods, Inc., which was purchased in 1979. Holdings also include a small amount of oil, some oil-search leases in Beaufort Sea, a logging operation, and a construction materials company in Anchorage.

Little remains of the old Indian cultures. Most of their ancient, highly developed craft skills have been forgotten, but a few have been revived for souvenir-hungry visitors to Alaska. Since 1966, when the Alaska State Council on the Arts was formed, a revival

on a higher artistic level has started. The council supports every
kind of art, artist, and art organization with money and opportunity. They cooperate with the State Museum, the Tlingit-Haida
Council, the Alaska Native Brotherhood, and others trying to save
and support native arts and crafts that are in danger of dying. If
dead they try resurrection, as with old Indian dances thought lost
forever. Lessons are now available in Aleut basket making and
Chilkat blanket weaving. Exhibitions are arranged so that beginning Eskimo carvers may see the best carving done in other
villages. For the first time in years native interest in the arts is
being kindled and linked with the highest artistic standards.

The universally popular Eskimos are the largest group of native
people in Alaska. After a long and almost disastrous population
decline, their numbers are increasing again. They are an able-
bodied, good humored, self-reliant, clever people, whose ancestors began to arrive in Alaska some 15,000 years ago. They live
along the shores of the Arctic and Bering seas, as well as in the
river deltas and in some cases up the river valleys, especially along

*Ivory carving is an important source of income to some of Alaska's most
remote Eskimos.*

the Colville, Noatak, Kobuk, and Kuskokwim rivers. They have always been a hunting people, following the fish and game animals with the seasons, but usually remaining in one general area. They hunted caribou, mountain sheep, and moose on the land; polar bear, seal, walrus, and whale at sea. Most village Eskimos, as opposed to those living in the big cities, still derive at least part of their living from the same animals hunted by their ancestors.

To some extent the Eskimos have always been fishermen, particularly on the Bering coast. Through the influence of the Russian American Company, of the Hudson's Bay Company, and of the Free Traders (as the independent competitors of the great fur trading companies are called), they became fur trappers.

North of the Arctic Circle, the majority of the Eskimos lived, for at least part of the year, on or near the coast. On the great inland prairie the population is now sparse; only 50 or 60 years ago it was inhabited by 10 or perhaps 20 times as many Eskimos as

Eskimo women at a Point Barrow whaling camp.

Whaling is still an important food source for Point Barrow Eskimos.

now. Then and earlier, coastal folk depended chiefly on seal and whale for food, and those of the interior lived on caribou, supplemented by birds, and fish from the inland lakes and rivers. In the mountains a comparatively few Eskimos lived mainly on sheep.

Seal, walrus, and whale oil provided coastal Eskimos with fuel and light. The inlanders used spruce, alder, and willow for fuel, and in their camps burned caribou tallow for light, or oil purchased from the coastal people in exchange for caribou hides and sheepskins. Once a year, most often in late winter, they would come down to the sea to hunt seals, to visit, and to trade.

Since their culture was so perfectly adapted to the climate of the Arctic, we tend to think of Eskimos as primarily an Arctic people. But more Eskimos live south of the latitude of Fairbanks than north of it.

The western and southern coasts of Alaska were in fairly close touch with the Russians and with other white men in the eighteenth century, and the interior similarly in the nineteenth. The northern coast had sporadic whalers 100 years ago but no resident trader until Charles D. Brower settled at Barrow in 1885 and established his famous trading post. Generally throughout Alaska, missionaries followed close on the heels of the traders.

The whalers and traders needed fresh meat for food and to ward off the dreaded scurvy. They had never heard of vitamins, but sea captains knew if they had fresh meat they and their crews would remain in good health. So they offered lures of every sort to get the Eskimos to hunt for them.

Soon after the first contact between the two peoples, Alaskan natives began to die in great numbers from diseases brought in by the whites. This was no doubt so throughout all of Alaska, but we know the story best from the Eskimos. The deadliness of the illnesses was due to their newness. No Eskimos had ever been exposed to them; therefore none had a natural immunity.

It is commonly believed that the worst killer that ever attacked the natives of the New World was smallpox. But insofar as we know the history of Alaska, the deadliest scourge was measles. There was an epidemic around the turn of the century that killed not less than one quarter of the people in any village we know about. This epidemic, according to a report we believe authentic, killed nearly 99 percent in one village, the only survivor being a girl of about six.

The second epidemic, a few years later, may have killed from 10 to 20 percent, the third killed only a few, and now the danger of measles to the Eskimos is not much greater than to us. Those who survived the first and second epidemics had an immunity against measles. Similar death rates from measles have been reported from tropical islands of the Pacific. Indeed a high mortality rate has been reported wherever measles had been previously unknown.

After measles, tuberculosis became the deadliest Eskimo disease and held the lead for decades. The U.S. Public Health Service is responsible for all native Alaskan medical needs. Since 1951 they have made great strides through education, new drugs like Isoniazid (INH), and additional hospitals in lowering the death rate from tuberculosis. Few natives *die* of TB now, thanks to chemotherapy, and the closing of the large TB wing of Anchorage's Alaska Native Hospital in 1972 because of lack of patients attests to the success of the war against the disease. Some think Eskimos always had TB but that it was kept in check by their wholesome food and old way of life. Others think, and this is the majority view, that Eskimos never had TB until it was introduced in historic times.

Under their "primitive" way of life Eskimos were free of many diseases that plague the white man. Apparently they formerly never had tooth decay, cancer, scurvy, or beriberi. As they shifted to the white man's way of life they acquired his diseases, too, and now the cancer rate among Eskimos is increasing, and alcoholism, mental illness, and suicide have become grave problems.

One of the few genuine benefits the whites brought to the Eskimos was the reduction of the death rate at childbirth for both mothers and children. Among primitive Eskimos it was not permissible for anyone to be present when a child was being born. The most custom permitted was that a woman's mother might be outside the house, shouting advice in to her daughter. In some areas, even this was taboo. But the Eskimos had one advantage, even in childbirth cases; the bacteria that cause infection were rare or absent. In the Arctic and sub-Arctic, almost every wound was formerly a clean wound.

The Eskimos and Indians of Alaska used to be wards of the government. They had no rights of citizenship, but the government was pledged to look after their welfare. In 1924 an act of Congress provided that "all non-citizen Indians, born within the territorial limits of the United States, shall be citizens," and that the granting of citizenship shall not in any way affect the right of an Indian to tribal or other property. Some have contended that the Eskimos are not Indians and would not come under this law, but it has been ruled that the law does apply to them. It would be strange if the law did not, for biologically and anthropologically they are of the same race.

Until their contact with Europeans, when births began to be recorded by missionaries and school teachers, the Eskimos did not know how old they were, except in a vague way, and considered it unimportant. They did not reckon age by years but by terms equivalent to "infant," "child," "youth," "adult." Primitive Eskimos counted by twenties, using both fingers and toes, where we use only the fingers; so that what corresponds to our 100, 10 times 10, is for them 400, 20 times 20. Occasionally some Eskimo might tell you that it was not possible to count higher than 400, but if you pressed him he could usually devise an extension.

To measure distance the Eskimos had nothing like our miles, but reckoned a journey in fractions of a day. If it was more than two days, they usually spoke in number of days.

An idea, or at least a word, which they did not have was "year." They spoke of spring, summer, autumn, and winter, and they reckoned years either in winters or in summers.

They had months in the sense of moons and usually knew that there were 13 in the complete cycle. But some of them would tell you that there were eight moons, nine moons, ten moons, according to what part of Alaska you were in, and then they would give the moonless period, which would be the summer, when the night was so bright that the moon could not be seen.

One of the strangest ideas to an Eskimo was that of our cardinal, or compass, points. Their directional thinking was not governed by the sun, but rather by the shoreline, for most of them were coastal people. So their directional phrases are "up the coast," "down the coast," "inland," and "out to sea." This has been confusing to those whites who did not know the language well, and you find in the vocabularies of Eskimo words copied down by average travelers that *nigerk* is a west wind, a south wind, and a north wind. *Nigerk* actually means a wind that blows up the coast. Similarly *kanangnak*, which has many meanings in published vocabularies, has only one meaning to the Eskimos. It is a wind from the sea, which may be north, south, east, or west, according to where you are. *Pingangnak* is a wind from the land, from "up there."

Eskimo children at Point Barrow.

To the old-timer, nothing brings home the irony of the phrase "the blessings of civilization" more than the appearance of a dentist in an Eskimo community. Fifty or seventy-five years ago he could not have earned a living in most villages because then every Eskimo had perfect teeth.

One of the marvels reported by early explorers was the way Eskimos could use their mouths as we use a vise or a claw hammer, as an extra tool. The strength of jaw and teeth was startling to us, as for instance their ability to pull a nail from a board with their teeth. In those days every tooth in every Eskimo head was sound. Sometimes the teeth were worn down to the gums with use, and occasionally even broken, but even then they never decayed. Nutritionists and anthropologists believe that where you find decayed teeth you have people who eat carbohydrates. When the white man introduced his food to the Eskimos—flour, sugar, hard bread, and molasses—he introduced tooth decay as well.

Around 1910 it was common in Alaska to meet people who could remember when they first heard of tooth decay and toothache. After shifting from the wholesome primitive diet to a white man's diet, it takes between four and ten years for the first cavities to appear. Village teachers instruct their pupils in tooth brushing and dental hygiene, but few of them mention that before Eskimos learned to brush their teeth they had no cavities, while now they have both toothache and cavities. The teeth of Eskimo villagers are just as bad as ours now; it is not uncommon, alas, to see young Eskimos in their thirties with complete dentures.

Eskimos are quick-witted, as any good ice hunter must be, for a quick death in cold water may be the price of a moment's hesitation. Their above-average intelligence, physical agility and endurance, navigational and hunting skills are combined with a wonderful sense of humor. They also have a remarkable capacity for appreciating, utilizing, and inventing things related to the mechanical arts.

One explorer tells of an Eskimo who possessed a dollar watch, which stopped after two years of use. Its owner proceeded to open the back of it and take it apart, piece by piece. After carefully cleaning each part he put it back together again so that it worked, although he had never before in his life taken a watch apart. Equally remarkable tales are told of their ingenuity in repairing outboard motor engines they have never seen before.

A completely mistaken but still popular belief is that all Eskimos live in igloos and that igloos are houses made of ice blocks. The Eskimo word igloo, better spelled iglu, is a general term meaning a temporary or permanent shelter for man or beast. Railway stations, cathedrals, tents, schoolhouses, and family dwellings are all igloos. A snow house is an igloo, too, but its own special name in the Mackenzie dialect is *apudyak*, from *apun*, the name for snow that is lying on the ground, as if ready to be cut into snow blocks for house building. In a few areas white men have told the natives that the word igloo should be reserved for a snow house, and some Eskimos now use it so.

A satisfactory snow house cannot be made of ice. Ice is a good conductor of temperature and would quickly transmit the outside chill indoors. Snow on the other hand is a poor conductor, which means it is an excellent insulator, thanks to the numerous air spaces captured within it. It can be cut in suitable blocks, is light to handle, and easy to shave and carve so that blocks fit neatly and lean at the proper angle. The colder the outdoor temperature, the warmer the inside of a snow house may be safely heated. Experienced travelers who have tried both tents and snow houses in winter camping invariably prefer the snow house as being more comfortable.

The dome-shaped house built of wind-packed snow blocks, held in place by ingenious engineering and gravity, was confined to an area in central Arctic Canada, east of the Mackenzie River. Use of the snow house extended eastward from there as far as one section of northwestern Greenland, where a small group known as the Polar Eskimos used it. But they were the only Greenlanders who did. South of the Polar Eskimos, only the earth—and the earth-and-stone—house was used. No Asiatic Eskimos ever used the snow dome structure either.

Alaskan Eskimos never used the snow houses for winter dwellings, as their neighbors to the east did. Some Alaskans knew of the existence of snow houses, a few having learned the skill from explorers or Canadian Eskimos, and then used them as traveling camps. Today all Alaskan Eskimos know about them, and most know how to build a good one. Many have learned through serving in the National Guard, or through reading books like Vilhjalmur Stefansson's *Arctic Manual*, which gives precise instructions and helpful drawings. And, of course, now they have all seen these snow houses in the movies or on television.

Primitive Eskimos in Alaska formerly built their houses of earth. North of the tree line, driftwood was substituted for local spruce to make the frames, and in some places the large bones of whales were used. In spring the Eskimo traditionally left his house to spend the summer in a tent. In the old days the tent was of skins; now it is apt to be of canvas.

One of the Eskimo's remarkable inventions was the way he used gravity in his house to keep the cold out and the warmth in. Winter houses, as made on the north coast of Alaska, had thick

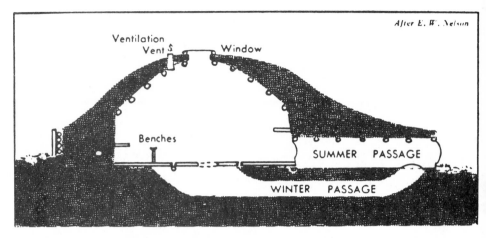

This schematic drawing shows how the air-capture principle is used in an Alaskan earth-and-wood house. In summer, the gut window is removed and a ground-level entrance is used. In winter, both window and entrance are closed and the house is entered through a passage by which buoyant warm air cannot escape. This passage is never closed all winter, unless a grid is used to keep out dogs.

earth walls and were always entered from below. The top of the door was always lower than the floor, and usually at the end of an alleyway. You entered the house by going down into a passage and up into the house at the other end. So long as the door was lower than the floor, it never needed to be shut, even at 50° F below zero. For cold air is heavier than warm air and cannot rise upward into a house already filled with warm air. Fresh air was provided by a small ventilator about four inches in diameter in the roof of the house. Cold air could enter from the door below only as warm air was permitted to escape through the ceiling vent. By widening or narrowing this vent, the Eskimo regulated the amount of heated air permitted to escape and cold air permitted to enter, thus controlling both the temperature and the ventilation of his house. If the house was too warm—and a normal temperature for an Eskimo house might be 80° or 90° F—the ventilator

The beach of an old Eskimo village was its main thoroughfare both in summer and in winter.

was opened wide; if too cool, it would be partially closed. A house with one room, big enough for two average families, needed only three seal oil lamps to keep the temperature at what we would consider more a Turkish bath than a comfortable room temperature.

The beach of an old Eskimo village was always its main plaza, the equivalent of our village green. It was the center of activity in both summer and winter. From the beach the hunter went sealing in his graceful kayak, and it was to the beach he returned. If successful, he was surrounded by interested and helpful neighbors. The animal would often be skinned and, if large, divided on the beach. Here, too, families starting off on a journey would pile their children, dogs, and household gear in the family umiak and wave a cheerful farewell as they paddled off. In winter, dog teams and sledges would depart and return via the beach.

Eskimos held views almost the opposite of ours about water and ice. To them ice was something friendly on which they could walk and hunt, which protected them from the treacherous waters below. We usually think of the water as being safe, the ice as treacherous. Eskimos seldom learned to swim. The waters of the Arctic Sea and Bering Sea are too cold, the mosquitoes too many and too hungry.

The Eskimo hunting canoe, the kayak, is no doubt the most seaworthy craft of its size. The spruce driftwood frames are shaped by hand. The pieces, instead of being nailed together, are lashed with wet rawhide, which draws tight as it dries. The sealskin covering fully envelops the boat except for a round deck opening just large enough to receive a man.

In some districts the boat's "manhole" merely fits the hunter's body rather snugly so as to give water little chance to enter; properly, the opening has a raised edge to which the Eskimo lashes the hem of his waterproof coat so that paddler and canoe become one. Water is prevented from entering not merely through the manhole but also through the sleeves and neck of the coat, which are tightly lashed. This hooded raincoat is made from

Eskimo boat frames were formerly shaped from driftwood; now imported lumber is often used.

A kayak overturns easily, but a good kayaker can right it with equal ease.

animal intestines, which are dried and sewn together to make a translucent, waterproof garment.

The kayak is about as steady on rough water as a man on a swaying tightrope. Its seaworthiness lies in the skill of the kayaker with his long double paddle, and in the boat and boatmen being a single unit.

Getting in and out of a kayak is a tricky art, accomplished by placing a pike pole or paddle across the boat, with one end resting on ice or on the beach. When a steady balance has been achieved, the kayaker ventures in or out. But don't try it on the basis of these instructions!

When an Eskimo boy is about 12 years old, his father will begin to teach him the difficult technique of handling a kayak, in those areas where they are still used. Long before this time, probably when he was six or seven, he learned to use a gun. He has killed small game and, if lucky, a seal. With his father he has gone on trips by dog team and perhaps made a short sledge journey or two by himself. But a kayak, unless expertly handled, is extremely dangerous. A boy must be serious-minded and industrious to master the art, for a mishap may end in drowning.

Instructions usually begin in a quiet lagoon sheltered from the rough surf. The kayak is so placed on the beach that while afloat on a few inches of water it can still be reached from dry land. The father then gets into the kayak and explains how to hold and manipulate the paddle, demonstrating each step as he tells of it. When this is thoroughly understood, father and son change places, and while the father holds on to the kayak, the boy imitates the motions of paddling. Step by step each maneuver is rehearsed and memorized before the boy takes to the water alone. Even then he is carefully watched and never goes far from shore at first. It takes years of practice to become an expert kayaker, but once the skill is acquired, kayak and paddler become practically unsinkable.

Accidents do occur in kayaks, but death usually results not from the kayak overturning once, because a good kayaker can right himself half a dozen times easily, but from the paddler being so

An expert kayaker must start his training early. The boy's father is usually the teacher—here he demonstrates first lessons in paddling.

fatigued from repeated capsizing that he is unable to right his boat.

While the kayak is a greater marvel of design, nearly the same admiration is due the larger umiak. This Eskimo boat, also skin-covered, is a dory type of craft and, like a dory, extremely seaworthy and capable of long voyages in rough weather. The average umiak is 35 or 40 feet long, can transport a two-ton load, yet is light enough for a man and his partner to carry. It is so strong and well fitted for rough handling that the Yankee shore whalers of northwestern Alaska, toward the end of the nineteenth century, exchanged their New Bedford whaleboats for umiaks in pursuing the bowhead whale. An ordinary wooden whaleboat is easily damaged even by small fragments of floating ice, while an umiak going at the same speed will not be harmed at all. A skin boat behaves somewhat like a footfall when it is struck. A thump is followed by a bouncy rebound. Should a blow be severe, the result might be a cracked rib that can be replaced at leisure, while a hole in the skin is easily patched with needle and thread.

Because it is light, has a flat bottom, and draws only a few inches of water, an umiak can venture safely into shallow places where ordinary boats are unable to navigate.

In summer, to prevent the skin covering of an umiak from decaying, it must be taken out of the water and dried at least every four days—preferably every three. This is easily accomplished. When a party camps for the night, the boat is taken out of the water and tilted on edge. If the weather is fair, the skins will be dry in the morning. Today many umiaks are canvas-covered.

Before the era of jet airplanes and tractor-pulled sledge trains, a dog sled was the only winter means of overland transportation in many parts of Alaska. As long as the ground was snow-covered, which might be for seven months of the year, dog teams were used by trappers, hunters, and mail carriers.

Although still used for sport racing now as well as utility, their numbers decrease each year. Snowmobiles, "ski-doos," and other motor driven vehicles have replaced them.

The so-called purebred Husky dog is a recent development of

A skin-covered umiak is light for its size and easily carried. Here Eskimo whalers are carrying theirs to an open lead. All wear goggles to prevent snow blindness.

The new and the old—a "ski-doo" and an Eskimo sled.

white dog breeders who carefully mate only dogs of a certain height, color, and fur, deciding beforehand the characteristics desired. These dogs are commonly bred and trained in Maine and New Hampshire. They are also used extensively by explorers both in the Arctic and Antarctic.

Sled dogs curl up to sleep in the snow.

Helping the dogs cross a difficult place.

Some early fur traders sent out by the Hudson's Bay Company to northern Canada were cockney Englishmen who dropped their *h*'s and inserted others where they didn't belong. They called Eskimos "Heskimos." An Eskimo dog was a "Heskimo" dog. "Heskimo" was soon shortened to "Hesky," which eventually became "Husky."

Wintertime, when it is a little too dark to do any real hunting, used to be a holiday time for Eskimos. Much of the dark season was spent making sledge journeys to visit back and forth with friends. Eskimo dog teams, once small, became larger in recent times, varying with the wealth of the owner and fashion in a given area. A lead dog is not necessarily the strongest member of a team, but he is usually the most intelligent, for he must interpret the driver's commands. Spirit is the mark of the leader, who may be of either sex and any size.

Thanks to his superior nose, a good leader can often find a trail, made invisible by drifting snow, and guide a lost driver safely home. Lazy dogs are rare, but not unknown. Most sled dogs love to pull and yelp excitedly as they are harnessed for a trip, much as a city dog dances with anticipation when his master appears with a leash that promises an outing.

Sled dogs are fed once a day and their ration usually is a dried salmon, but they will eat almost anything if they are used to it— seal, caribou, or goose. Dog fights that break out must be stopped immediately, for they may result in the death or maiming of a valuable dog. For this reason dogs are seldom allowed to run loose. After a day's work they are tethered to stakes, out of reach of each other. Good sled dogs are workers rather than pets; for doing their particular job these tough, handsome beasts are unsurpassed.

Eskimo sleds can carry from 500 to 1,000 pounds of load. Formerly, an Eskimo, unless ill, never rode on the sled. He was much more likely to be up front giving the dogs a hand over a rough spot. In extremely cold weather, if a sled is allowed to stop, the runners will freeze fast in the snow. Then it must be rocked loose with a "gee pole," the steering device attached to the right-hand sledge runner. White men introduced a kind of rude brake on the back of the sled. It will not stop a runaway team, but is useful for slowing the sled when going downhill.

Some think Eskimos were able to survive in the Arctic because they hardened themselves to it, and so could stand it better than white men. But Eskimos never endured or suffered cold if they could help it; they protected themselves from it in many ingenious ways. They wore truly marvelous, cold-proof clothing, which kept them warm however extreme the cold. An Eskimo in his old-style clothing could don a ten-pound caribou skin outfit in January and sit still comfortably outdoors all afternoon while fishing through the ice at 50° F below zero.

A Point Hope Eskimo youth in a coat that has the skin side outside and the fur side inside.

Before the white man's influence became strong, Eskimo cold-weather dress consisted of two suits of caribou skin; the inner one was worn with the fur side in, and the other with the fur side out. Each suit was made up of coat, or *attigi*, and breeches that tied about the waist with a drawstring; there are no buttons or buttonholes on truly Eskimo clothing. Both undershirt and outer coat had hoods exposing the cheeks and forehead but protecting the ears. Boots and mittens completed the costume. Inner and outer coats were worn loose, outside the trousers. If the weather became so windy that the garment flapped, a belt was passed around the undercoat to prevent cool air from coming up inside.

It is not enough to own a suit of Eskimo clothing to ensure comfortable protection from the cold. It is also necessary to know how to wear it and take care of it. Dry snow and hoarfrost must always be carefully removed before entering a warm house.

When caribou skins have been dried and scraped they are soft and free from odors. Then the highly skilled Eskimo women would fashion them into garments, each of which was a tailor-made work of art. Eskimo seamstresses used to make what is probably the only true waterproof seam in the world. Our bootmakers think a seam cannot be waterproof and usually rub oil or wax into their needle holes. But if an Eskimo sewer saw you rubbing oil on her boot seam she would feel insulted. When a waterboot was finished she would inflate it like a balloon, twist the mouth, and wait for a few minutes to see if any air was escaping. She would hold the seam to her cheek to detect the slightest leak of air, or near a lamp or candle flame to notice the slightest flicker. Caribou sinew was originally used for thread. When a new pair of boots was about to be worn they would be dampened and the sinew would swell, making the seam tight.

Observing the white people's fashions, Eskimos were quick to adopt first one, then another, item of their clothes. Eventually the miracle of the mail-order catalog reached every village, however remote. Summer dress throughout the Eskimo world then underwent a change. Formerly skin clothing was worn the year round—it was all they had. Now cotton dresses and shirts, rubber boots,

Point Barrow seamstresses still make Eskimo skin boots, but their igloos are now heated by natural gas.

blue jeans, and plaid lumber jackets are as popular with them as with us. For summer wear our clothing is more comfortable than theirs; but in winter theirs is far better than ours. Nothing we can offer is nearly as good in extreme cold as an Eskimo caribou skin coat, or an Eskimo-style sealskin waterboot. These two items at least seem destined to survive every onslaught of fashion. An important reason for Eskimos to adopt our clothing is that many now work for wages and have no time to hunt caribou and seals; so there are no skins for making clothing. The fur clothing offered for sale in Alaskan shops is neither good in quality nor inexpensive.

Eskimo mothers used to, and many still do, carry their babies on their backs inside their coats, the child sitting pick-a-back fashion with its little legs around the mother's waist. A belt to prevent it from slipping down was passed under the child in back, brought forward, and fastened in front over the mother's breast (see page 62). If the child was young, it was naked and completely hidden from view inside the coat. If older, and the weather mild,

Eskimo mother and child.

it might be lightly clad and its head might protrude from the top of the coat.

Unless his parents are getting all too disagreeably "civilized," an Eskimo child is never punished. The reason is not that Eskimos love their children more than other parents, but rather what they used to believe about the soul.

According to their ancient theory, a child is born with a soul and a body that are equally small and weak. It seemed obvious to an Eskimo that the child would never get along if it did not have a more experienced and wiser soul to look after it. The first thing a mother did after her child was born was to pronounce a spell and summon the spirit of some person who had recently died.

The Eskimos have no sex indication in their language. They have no pronouns like "he" or "she" in English; they have no sex inflection for adjectives and nouns such as you find in Latin or German. This may be why it made no difference in their thinking whether the spirit summoned was that of a man or woman. In some districts it had to be the spirit of a near relative who had recently died. In another area it might be the spirit of the last person who had died, irrespective of relationship.

It was the Eskimo view of the spirits of the dead that they are strongest just after they first enter the newborn child, and gradually become weaker as the child grows up. Correspondingly, the inborn soul of the child was thought to be weakest at birth and to gradually become stronger. They believed that when a child is very young its thinking is done for it exclusively by the soul of the dead person, the child's inborn soul having little or no control. If, for instance, a child cried for the scissors it was, in Eskimo opinion, the judgment of the guardian soul that the child ought to have the scissors.

This gave the parents two reasons for yielding. In the first place, it was unthinkable that they were wiser than the guardian spirit. If they refused they would surely offend the guardian, who would thereupon leave the child. With nothing but its own incompetent soul to take care of it, the baby would suffer one misfortune after another. If a man's ears stuck out at the wrong angle or if his nose

Eskimos do rub noses! But it is an affectionate gesture used between young children and older women.

had a strange shape it was usual to hear people remark that his parents must have punished him when he was young.

According to the old Eskimo way of thinking, during the first few years of a child's life, you were distinctly speaking to the soul of the dead when you addressed the child. Therefore it was customary for those related to the dead to address a baby in terms of that relationship. For instance, if my grandmother's soul had been given to a small boy, I would call him "grandmother" whenever I spoke to him or about him. A mother talking to her baby girl might call her "father," if it was her father's soul which had been given to her daughter. Very confusing to non-Eskimos!

While Eskimos are now Christian and not supposed to believe in guardian spirits, it remains true to this day that Eskimo children are practically never punished physically or forbidden anything.

It is commonly believed that primitive people have simple languages, but linguists tell us the opposite is often true. This is confirmed by the Eskimo language, which (as we said earlier) some believe to be the hardest language in the world to learn. The active daily vocabulary has more than 10,000 words, most of which are nouns and verbs. Adjective and adverb meanings are supplied by inflection. The inflections are so numerous and complicated that one noun can be written in more than 1,000 forms, each with a separate, precise meaning of its own. A verb can have even more forms than a noun!

The structure of Eskimo is so different from English that you must learn a new way of thinking as well as a new vocabulary if you want to speak the language.

For instance, the average American, who wants to learn the language, seeks out an Eskimo who speaks English and, taking care not to be misunderstood, he will hold a knife in his hand and ask, "What is your word for 'knife'?" The Eskimo will answer "*savik*." "And what is your word for 'big'?" is the next question, whereupon the answer, in Colville River dialect, will be "*angirok*." "Now," thinks the white man, "I know how to say 'big knife,'" but as a matter of fact he doesn't know at all, for the Eskimo does not say "big knife" by attaching the adjective for "big" to the word for "knife." Instead he inflects the word for knife by adding a syllable, in this case *pa*, which means big. A big knife is not as we might think "*savik angirok*" or "*angirok savik*"; it is "*savipak*." We are accustomed to prefixes and suffixes; the Eskimo also use *in*fixes. That is, they take a word apart and insert a syllable in the middle (rather than at the beginning or end) to alter the meaning.

There are nine cases in Eskimo and they, as in Greek, have singular, dual, and plural forms, giving you theoretically 27 variants of a word, before you add any infixes. (However, it is difficult to make out nine forms in the dual.)

To get an idea of how the inflections work, take the word *iglu*, which means a temporary or permanent shelter of any sort. *Iglupak* means a large house; *iglunguak*, a make-believe or playhouse; *iglorak*, a wooden house; *iglukuk*, a ruined house; *igluliak*, a house that someone built; *iglulik*, that which contains houses, as an island that is inhabited; *iglutun*, like a house; and so on for several hundred variants of one word *iglu*.

The noun is simple compared with the verb. No man has ever worked out the number of possible different ways in which a single Eskimo verb may be used, but an experienced Eskimo linguist has estimated it at a minimum of 3,000.

Under primitive conditions Eskimos always shared their food. No one went hungry while others had plenty; they were well-fed or hungry together. Unlike the Indians, Eskimos had no chiefs, slaves, or aristocrats; in fact, they had no caste. No one held office. No man could order another to do his bidding. Men of judgment and skill were looked up to and consulted because of their superior wisdom or talent, not because of rank. There was equality between men and women; a husband could not *order* his wife to do anything, or vice versa. All common problems of these essentially gentle people were discussed amicably and often at great length. Their often-reported happiness seems to have been the result of good health and of a fortunately natural attitude toward life and death.

Relatively little of the old ways remains today except the Eskimos' remarkably cheerful spirit and the fine quality of their relations with each other and the outside world. The hunting way of life is fading, but any Eskimo who can, still hunts on the weekend.

Nunivak Island children.

Eskimos on the back of a small white whale, or beluga.

The mechanical skills reported by early explorers have enabled the Eskimos to become excellent mechanics, tractor drivers, carpenters, and radio operators. There are Eskimo plane dispatchers, nurses, soldiers, businessmen, artists, writers, hotel- and storekeepers, legislators, newspaper editors, and teachers. For many hundreds of years, existence was so difficult for Eskimos that only the quick-witted, sharp-sighted hunter with good judgment and quick reflexes managed to survive. The present-day Eskimos are his descendants.

In the first century of his contact with the white man, the Arctic Eskimo never stood in awe of Western civilization. For in northernmost Eskimo territory the white man was uncomfortable, if not helpless, without Eskimo clothing, Eskimo guides, Eskimo dogs and sledges, and his food had to be shipped in from the outside. The Eskimo was, and felt himself to be, the superior man. Today many Eskimo ideals have been exchanged for those of the white man. Although he is generally quicker, more observant, and more patient than the white man, the Eskimo no longer feels superior.

Among Alaskan natives there is a new surge of pride in all things

Indian and Eskimo. This concern for cultural identity is a source of support for peoples who have lost dominance over their lands and a formerly close rapport with family and groups. Reminders of past greatness help them to endure present poverty and the difficulties of living in a white man's world. Now when so few native children speak the languages of their parents, there is suddenly a hunger to learn those languages. There is also a rising desire on the part of the parents to preserve and hand on to their children as much of their ancient heritage as possible.

According to Michael Krauss, Chief of Linguistic Staff, Alaskan Native Language Center, Alaska contains two great North American language families, the Eskimo-Aleut and the Indian Na-Dene. Both have spread far beyond Alaska, the Inupiaq-Eskimo to Canada and Greenland, and Athabascan Na-Dene to Canada and southwestern United States. Within these two families there is considerable diversity. The Eskimo includes both Yupik and Inupiaq dialects, and Na-Dene includes Tlingit and Eyak and about 10 of the 30 Athabascan languages. Two other Indian languages only marginally part of the Alaskan scene are Tsimshian and Haida.

The period of Russian domination in Alaska from 1825–1865 was not only more beneficial in the history of Alaskan native languages and cultures than earlier Russian periods, but also more beneficial than any of the following American periods. In 1824 Ivan Veniaminov, a very capable and humane missionary, arrived in the Aleutians and brought with him a period of enlightenment and benign Russian influence in the colony. The Russian Orthodox Church and its educational system brought a type of culture to the native languages. The first book printed in any Alaskan native language was the revised Aleut catechism, published in 1834 under Veniaminov, who in 1826 had adapted the Slavonic alphabet to Aleut. Widespread literacy developed at first in connection with the church and church school activities but also spread to secular writing. These traditions were beginning to flourish at the time of the sale of Alaska in 1867.

At that time a large number of natives naturally knew Russian,

Eskimo boy with fish-drying racks.

but probably all Alaskan natives still spoke their native languages. The Russian influence on native languages may be measured by the number of Russian loan words still in use today. In Aleut there are about 400 Russian loans; in Alutiiq over 350; in Tanaina over 350; but Tlingit has only 9, a linguistic reflection of Tlingit resistance to the Russians, which was matched by their better-known military resistance. Even with the assimilation into their own native languages of Russian loan words, Alaskan native languages are "purer" than most European languages and English. In surviving the Russian period, several Alaskan languages were in fact strengthened by the development of literature and literacy.

By the early 1900s American schools, and probably by then also most mission schools, completely forbade the use of native languages. Children were forbidden and often physically punished "for their own good" for speaking their own language at school. Their teachers, usually from the lower 48, often had no knowledge of either native languages or native cultures. In the already literate Aleut area, the last of the native Aleut religious schools, which taught both written Aleut and Russian, was forcibly closed in 1912.

In 1967 a federal bilingual education act was passed, permitting for the first time instruction in languages other than English to children in public-supported American schools. This law did not require that children whose primary language was other than English be provided with bilingual education, but only opened the door for it to be permitted where there was a need or demand for it. In 1970 the Bureau of Indian Affairs, which was still operating many schools in the state, together with the State-Operated School System, was persuaded to experiment with bilingual education in four Central Yupik schools. This was the first time in about 60 years that Alaskan native children were taught in their native language.

The Native Claims Settlement Act, which brought sweeping changes to the state, also affected education. Six months after its enactment, encouraged by the dramatic success of the bilingual education effort in the Central Yupik area, the Alaska State Legislature enacted, on June 9, 1972, a pair of bills on behalf of Alaskan native languages. One bill made Alaska one of the first states to require that children be introduced to education in their native language. It stipulated that every school with 15 or more students whose dominant language was other than English must have a teacher who is fluent in the language, a program, and written materials. Bureau of Indian Affairs schools were not required to follow state regulation, but since 1972 they have all been gradually transferred to state control. Today the law affects all the children in schools in Alaska.

At the same time the state legislature passed the Alaska Bilingual Education bill, it also established the Alaska Native Language Center at the University of Alaska for developing writing and literature for bilingual programs and for training writers and teachers in these languages. The center's budget is limited, as is its staff. It cannot train all the needed teachers and produce all the necessary school books. It has, however, trained the first generation of teachers and writers of most of the languages and produced the first books.

Michael Krauss, a gifted linguist, is a chief force behind the language center. He has been in Alaska since 1960 and has studied almost all the native Alaskan languages. More important, he is an active promoter and cultivator of Alaskan languages. Rather than embalm a dying language, he prefers, he says, to keep it alive. He turns talented students into teachers, and several have become his assistants. He knows how to involve, interest, and excite natives with bi- or trilingual skills to join his "movement."

The staff of the Alaska Native Language Center, directed by Professor Krauss and Professor Irene Reed, consists of 11 full-time linguists, some of them Alaskan natives working on their own languages, and about as many native language specialists who work with the linguists on a part-time basis. Many of the staff travel to villages and towns holding literacy workshops, working with school curricula, training teachers, and assisting native writers. Another activity of the center is the maintenance of an archival library with holdings that include almost every printed document and much of the unpublished material that has been written in or on any Alaska native language. Its collection of 4,000 items is both record and resource for language work in the state.

IV / FACT AND FABLE

ALASKA IS A LAND OF EXTREMES—of the very old and the very new, of ancient Eskimo and Indian cultures and modern pulp mills and rocket ranges. Here you will find, side by side, glaciers and strawberries, dog teams (although they are dwindling in number) and airplanes. A skin boat, the design of which has not changed for a thousand years, is fitted with the latest model outboard motor.

The state of Alaska contains a confusing variety of climates and terrains. Between rainy southeastern Alaska and the northernmost treeless Arctic slope are magnificent snow-clad mountains, vast forests, broad prairies. Alaska has the third largest river in North America, the meandering Yukon, placed by its length and drainage basin after the Mississippi and Canada's Mackenzie. It has innumerable small lakes but no large ones.

One of the commonest mistakes made about Alaska is that it is a frigid country, so chilled that there are no summers. But two thirds of Alaska lies below the Arctic Circle, and even at Point Barrow, its north tip, the lowest winter temperature is slightly above the lowest records of North Dakota, Wyoming, and Montana. In central Alaska the maximum heat of summer is about equal to that of New York City. The U.S. Weather Bureau has

Close-up views of different kinds of glaciers are seen on a tourist trip to the Juneau Ice Fields.

recorded temperatures of 100° F in the shade at Fort Yukon, just north of the Arctic circle, 99° at Fairbanks, just south of the Circle, and similar highs for other places. The heat in the Arctic is usually humid. In summer the days grow longer and longer until, for a short period in northerly latitudes, they are 24 hours long, and the sun never sets. The heat is continuous; there is no cooling-off period as in the tropics. While the summer season is much shorter in the Arctic than in the tropics, without the relief of cool nights it seems harder to endure.

We *expect* Alaska to be cold and are not disappointed. The winter of 1971 was a bitter one and on January 23 all Alaskan and U.S. records for extreme cold were broken when a temperature of −80° F was recorded at Prospect Creek, a site in the foothills of the Brooks Range on the Prudhoe Bay–Valdez pipeline. Nothing colder has been recorded.

Unless you have been in the north in summertime, it is hard to visualize and impossible to describe the terrific number of mosquitoes that exist. Formerly, no European traveler dared move into the bush country, or out upon the prairies, without a headnet, gloves, and heavy clothing lashed tightly at wrist and ankle to protect him against the pests. Thanks to the invention during World War II of several effective mosquito repellents, one can now wear light clothing without being at the mercy of biting insects.

Mosquitoes do not breed as well in a lake as in a swamp; they prefer many small puddles of water. In most of the Yukon Valley, when you dig below the surface a few inches, the ground is permanently frozen. Last winter's snow water and yesterday's rain cannot penetrate downward through the hard-as-concrete frost but stays on the surface to form innumerable swamps, each an ideal breeding place for mosquitoes.

Permafrost underlies the northern two thirds of Alaska. Experts tell us it occurs beneath one fifth of the entire earth's land surface. Half of Canada and much of the northern Soviet Union have permafrost. Wherever it occurs, lack of underground drainage results in thousands or, more likely, millions of lakes, ranging in size from small puddles to many square miles. When you fly over permafrost country it has a typical look—half or even more of the ground below is covered by lakes of all sizes and shapes. These provide landing places for pontoon planes in summer and wheel- or ski-equipped aircraft in winter.

It is no accident that Alaskans fly more than any other people in the world. The distances between cities are often great, the highways are few, and the terrain is various, rugged, and difficult. Often an airplane is the only means of reaching what would otherwise be an isolated place. By 1981 Alaska had a certified pilot for every 38 residents and one in 55 Alaskans owned his own plane. The state carries more passengers and flies more cargo tonnage per year than any other state.

Small pontoon planes are a common sight in Alaska.

The Great Circle polar routes to the Orient can save as many as 4,000 miles on flights between Europe and Asia by flying directly. Anchorage and Fairbanks have become international airports, with most aviation companies now offering flights to Asia via the forty-ninth state.

Along the suburban lake shores of Anchorage you will see rows of neatly moored pontoon planes awaiting their owner-pilots. Most are small craft that take off or land on any of Alaska's numberless lakes. Families living in Alaska's largest city use them to "get away from the congestion of city life." Planes bring spare parts, machinery, mail, fresh food, and relief workmen to remote mining and oil developments. They pick up and deliver trappers, fishermen, scientists, tourists, or weekend campers. They taxi doctors, nurses, and patients in and out of the bush and permit a minister to visit the farthest borders of his parish. Nowadays prospecting for metals and oil is done from the air; so is mapping,

Dramatic mountain scenes unfold on the flight to Anchorage from the south.

in a fraction of the time formerly required. Children go to school by plane in Alaska, salesmen visit their customers, and some prosperous women at Point Barrow are said to fly south regularly to Fairbanks, a 1,000-mile round trip, to shop and have their hair done.

In tiny, distant villages, the bush pilot still plays an important role. Usually one man does all the flying to and from a small village. He knows the terrain by heart and has made friends with the local weather. He will fly in weather other flyers would not dare attempt. He is a combination mailman, ambulance driver, personal shopper, and Santa Claus. Sometimes he is the only link between the village and the outside world. Of necessity he is their confidant; he is their newsbearer, and usually is adored by the villagers. If he has any unusual personality traits they are discussed with relish and woven into a kind of folklore that follows him for the rest of his life.

There are two railroads in all of Alaska: the Alaska Railroad, whose main line operates from Seward to Fairbanks, and the White Pass and Yukon, which runs through only 20 miles of Alaska on its way from Skagway to Whitehorse, in Canada's Yukon Territory. The Alaska Railroad is government-operated and has 537 miles of track. In summertime the daylight trip from Fairbanks to Anchorage is a favorite with tourists, for it cuts through the heart of Alaska, with magnificent scenery all the way.

In 1982 the federal government wanted to divest itself of ownership of the Alaska Railroad. A dispute between the governments of Alaska and the United States has arisen over whether or not it should be given as a gift to the state. The realization that Alaska's state government has become wealthy from royalties and taxes on oil wells is the thrust behind Congress's insistence that the state pay for the railroad. No provision has been made for the railroad in the 1983 proposed federal budget. The lack of federal funds to run it may spur a decision as to what will become of the Alaska Railroad.

One of the most popular stops on the Alaska Railroad is at Mount McKinley National Park, where the chief attraction is the mighty mountain the Indians call *Denali*, meaning "home of the sun." Mount McKinley is one of the most dramatic sights in a land that abounds in stunning scenery. The light tan granite mass, crown of the Alaska Range, climbs upward to a height of almost four miles! No other mountain in the world rises so far above its own base. The upper two-thirds of the peak is permanently snow-covered and often takes on a pinkish glow at sunrise and sunset.

McKinley Park, covering over 3,000 square miles, was created by an act of Congress in February 1917. In 1978 a presidential proclamation designated 56 million acres of federal land in Alaska as national monuments. One of them, Denali National Monument, expanded McKinley Park by 3.89 million acres. Later, an act of Congress changed the name of McKinley Park to Denali National Park, reverting to the earlier traditional Indian name. It is the northernmost and fourth largest U.S. national park. All three larger national parks are also located within Alaska; Wrangell–Saint Elias National Park is the largest, followed by Gates of the Arctic National Park and Katmai National Park. Denali Park's snow-capped peaks and grinding glaciers slope down into spruce-forested valleys. The park abounds in wildlife. Caribou, giant Alaska moose, handsome white Dall mountain sheep, grizzly bear, wolf, wolverine, and lynx are some of the animals that might be seen by a lucky tourist from a train window as the railroad speeds through the park.

When the Alaska Road Commission was formed in 1905, there were less than a dozen miles of passable wagon road in Alaska. Today the famous Alaska Highway connects Canada with Alaska. Almost 1,600 miles long, it was completed during a wartime emergency in November 1942 thanks to the almost superhuman efforts of both Canadian and American military and civilian construction men. As soon as it was finished, in a record-breaking eight months, military equipment began streaming in from the States through Canadian Edmonton and Whitehorse, to Fair-

Horseshoe Lake in Mount McKinley National Park is typical of the grandeur and beauty of the state.

banks, the Alaskan terminus. After the war, tourists followed, growing in numbers each year. The 298.7 miles in Alaska are paved today.

In 1948, spurred by a tense world political situation, the U.S. military examined Alaska again. Her geographical position gave her new value in an atomic and hydrogen bomb age. Facing the Arctic Sea on the north, almost touching Siberia on the west, and bounding the North Pacific to the south, Alaska stood virtually undefended. Huge costly military installations were built, along with new and improved roads with which to service them.

The current highway system includes a 4,692-mile network of all-weather paved roads. They connect the ice-free ports of Valdez, Seward, and Haines with interior Alaska's principal cities and military installations, as well as with the lower 48 states. A secondary system of 3,654 miles connects farming and industrial areas to the main network.

A relatively new string to the Alaskan transportation bow is the Alaska Marine Highway System. It operates the Southeastern and Southwestern Alaska ferry systems, providing transportation for the Alaskans who live in the coastal and island areas of the state with the equivalent of a land highway system. The beautiful, protected waterways of the Alexander Archipelago offer a natural communication and travel route both for Alaskans and the growing number of tourists. The Southwestern System is served by two ferries, the Bartlett and the Tustumena. The former carries 165 passengers and serves Valdez, Cordova, and Whittier, while the latter carries 200 serving Seward, Homer, Seldovia, Port Lions, Kodiak, Valdez, and Cordova. The seven vessels of the Southeastern System move vehicles and people between fourteen ports: Ketchikan, Metlakatla, Hollis (offering access to Craig, Klawock, and Thorne Bay), Wrangell, Petersburg, Kake, Sitka, Angoon, Pelican, Hoonah, Tenakee Springs, Juneau, Haines, and Skagway. Regular service is also provided from Prince Rupert, British Columbia, and Seattle, Washington. Its fleet ranges in size from the *Columbia*, with a capacity of 1,000 passengers, to the *Chilkat*, which accommodates only 75. The ferries are extremely popular in summer but operate at a loss in winter.

Stern-wheelers were once a familiar sight on the Yukon River.

In recent years, as the speed and range of airplanes increased, so did our understanding of Great Circle air routes. The Arctic or Polar Sea, surrounded by the world's most powerful nations, acquired a new—and to some, ominous—importance. The old east-west air routes are as dated as biplanes. The new routes lead north or cross the Arctic regions diagonally. If hostile planes ever approach our land, we believe they will come not from the Atlantic or Pacific but from beyond the North Pole.

In response to this new orientation the Distant Early Warning Line of radar stations was created in 1952. Known more familiarly as the DEW Line, the function of its numerous outposts, ringing northern Canada and Alaska, is to warn of the approach of enemy planes. Building the DEW Line resulted in the largest invasion of the Arctic in terms of men, ships, materials, and equipment in the history of the Northland. Every known means of transportation was utilized, and a few new ones invented. By ship, by plane, by long tractor-driven sledge trains, by river barge, and by giant new rubber-wheeled vehicles that could travel over snowy roadless tundra in summer and winter—men and materials converged on North America's northernmost continental shore. Hampered by the need for developing special methods to deal with short summers, ice-choked waterways, permafrost, muskeg (a thick, spongy, waterlogged carpet of mosses and sedges), cold temperatures, and humid summer heat, the engineers pushed on. The successful completion of the DEW Line in the surprisingly short time of a year was a victory over stupendous obstacles.

A hazard associated with life in the far north is the uncertainty

of radio reception. Radios have a way of suddenly, without warning, going dead. Sometimes, too, sunspot activity and noisy atmospheric static will blot out the signal. Since such interruptions might be disastrous in wartime, the Defense Department, as part of the general fortification of Alaska, built a huge communications network designed to keep us in touch with the farthest Alaskan outposts, whatever the weather. The code name of the project, while secret, was White Alice, and it still bears the name. Alaska Integrated Communications Enterprise became "Alice," and "White" described Alaska in winter. Originally it was to be called

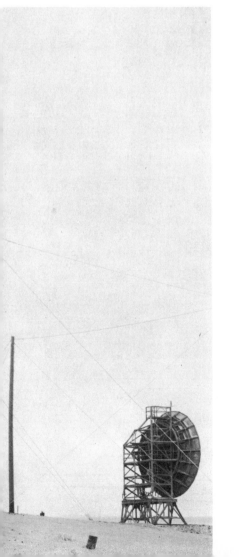

The buildings and equipment of a DEW Line station form an interesting pattern.

Alice White, but then an actress with the same name was discovered!

On November 30, 1956, the first link of White Alice's chain of stations was finished. Each of the 47 stations (later expanded to some 60 sites) was equipped to receive and transmit signals, using a method of radio relay never before used on such a large scale. Good telephone and telegraphic communications were maintained between stations, whether skies were stormy or clear. Huge scoop-shaped, 60-foot-high antennas, each weighing 100 tons, were used to beam signals into the troposphere, the seven- to ten-mile layer of air that extends upward from the earth. In the troposphere the signals were "scattered," and only a tiny fraction of the energy sent out arrived at the receiving antenna. Here it was amplified until intelligible. Identical antennas, spaced at distances of up to 200 miles, received the signals and retransmitted them if necessary.

White Alice was designed primarily to enable the air force to keep in touch with radar outposts, but all government departments, civilian telephone, and telegraph agencies, as well as the

A White Alice station in the Matanuska Valley.

For centuries Alaska's rivers were her only highways.

people of Alaska, benefited in peacetime from the system.

In 1976 RCA Alascom took control of White Alice from the air force. Finding the system was a large energy consumer and required a small army to maintain, RCA began work on larger satellite earth stations to replace it. White Alice, which was state-of-the-art communications technology in the 1950s, is obsolete today.

For centuries Alaska's principal interior highways were rivers. In summer they served as liquid avenues for Eskimo kayak and umiak and Indian canoe. Later the white man introduced paddle-wheeled, wood-burning steamboats and other craft. After fall freeze-up, rivers are transformed into broad ice highways on which formerly dog teams, horse teams, and more recently motor and tracked vehicles would travel. More freighting is being done throughout the north by caterpillar tractors, or "cats" as they are called, pulling long trains of heavily loaded freight sledges. In building the DEW Line, a new kind of vehicle was introduced. This was a huge houselike truck, with giant rubber-tired wheels, taller than a man, which rolled effortlessly across the roadless, snow-covered frozen muskeg. Teams of drivers ate and slept in them, taking turns driving. Snow cats and skidoos are now common, but hovercraft and Rolligons, vehicles with huge air-filled rollers, are the vehicles of the future. As mentioned earlier, heavy-wheeled vehicles will kill tundra vegetation and begin to melt the permafrost below.

A vehicle that may offer one solution to the protection of the environment and especially the fragile permafrost, which is damaged by conventional vehicles, is a curious-looking "truck without wheels, a tractor without tracks," called a Rolligon. Instead of wheels or tracks the Rolligon has wide, big, thin-walled, ultra-low pressure air bags. It can operate in roadless areas without tearing up the vegetation cover as tractors or heavy

The extraordinary-looking Rolligon travels anywhere in all seasons and every kind of weather and doesn't damage the fragile Arctic vegetation.

The hovercraft offers one more solution to Alaska's transportation problems.

trucks do. It travels easily in summer across swamps, sand, waterlogged muskeg and tundra; and in winter through snow and even along frozen river beds without danger, since the weight it carries, more than ten tons, is evenly divided on its eight huge rolling air bags. These roller bags replace wheels and lightly press the vegetation cover instead of cutting into and wounding it permanently as other vehicles do. The 35-foot-long Rolligon travels easily across rough country, steep hills, the soft rubber bags conforming to whatever unevenness is encountered. Rolligons have demonstrated that they can travel in midwinter without snowplow assistance and that they can perform ordinary construction work without harming the environment.

Another vehicle that seems hopeful for safe Arctic use is the hovercraft, which operates on a cushion of air either on land or water.

Every tiny village in Alaska, even a lone wilderness camp, has a

shortwave radio receiving and sending set. The two-way radio is
vital for survival in many parts of Alaska, especially the sparsely
settled areas. It combines the virtues of newspaper, telephone,
telegraph, and a visit across the back fence with a neighbor. It is
the link with civilization, the source of help in troubled times, the
bearer of tidings, good and bad. If a plane is overdue, you first
hear of it on the radio. If a listener has news of it, he reports. If
hours go by without word, rescue plans take form and are put into
action.

Sometimes homey messages are heard through the innumerable privately owned two-way radios. Recipes and gossip are

exchanged. Chess games are played, a move or two a day, by players hundreds of miles apart. Strangers in the area are sure to be mentioned, their business and personalities discussed, and, usually unbeknownst to them, their movements will be followed with friendly interest.

The shortwave radio dispenses medical information to isolated villages, especially in emergencies, where a plane would be unlikely to arrive in time, or when weather prevents the flight. Operations have been performed by schoolteachers and others with little or no knowledge of surgery, step by step, according to instructions from a doctor who may be 1,000 miles away and who

An Indian fishing camp on the Tanana River.

calmly, quietly asks questions and gives directions. Countless babies have been delivered by this unusual hospital of the air waves.

A better, far more sophisticated method of dispensing medical information began in the early 1970s, when the world's first regional satellite communication network began operations. Twenty-five Alaskan towns and villages, many of them remote, are able to get quick, accurate diagnostic and treatment information from staff members of the big city hospitals. The connecting link that makes it possible is NASA Satellite ATS-1. The research for this project was done at the University of Alaska, and it was financed through a federal grant from the National Center for Biomedical Communications.

Weather reports, by which the aviator lives, are broadcast on shortwave radio at regular intervals and by request. Nowhere in the world does there seem to be so much talk of weather as in Alaska. Good weather means flights on time, mail, groceries, machinery, and people delivered on schedule. Bad weather means waiting and more waiting, no mail, no flights, boredom, frustration. Where the plane is one's only link with "outside," talk about cold fronts, cloud ceilings, fog, moon, and visibility is highly pertinent.

In 1969 oil and gas surpassed fisheries as Alaska's second most populous industry. The federal government ranked first! Alaska nevertheless leads all other states in the value of its fish products, $597 million in 1979, and salmon is still the most valuable fish.

Long before the coming of the white man, Alaska's salmon provided the prime source of food for Indians living on the coast and inland along rivers. In 1878 the first commercial canneries were established, and within the 50-year period following, according to former governor and senator Ernest Gruening, Alaska became the world's greatest salmon producer. Salmon surpassed gold mining as the major industry; the salmon industry represented the largest capital investment, showed the biggest annual financial yield, and was the greatest employer of labor.

At the end of the 1930s the size of the annual salmon runs for the first time began to decline sharply. Some say overfishing was the cause; others blame insufficient or poorly enforced conservation measures. It seems to have been a complex combination of biological, social, economic, and other forces. Nevertheless, the salmon runs began increasing with the 1979 commercial catch of 467.7 million pounds, the largest since 1941. During late summer and fall, millions of salmon still swim in Alaskan waters on their way to spawn.

Salmon are hatched in fresh water, where they remain two years, and then descend to the sea. When they migrate outbound they are only a few inches long. They grow rapidly in salt water, and two or three years later, fully grown, they each return to the stream where it was born, to spawn and die. It is on this homeward migration that the fish are taken for commercial purposes.

Formerly salmon roe was always discarded during processing, but in the 1960s a market was found for it in Japan, and now it adds considerably to the value of the salmon catch. Salmon fishing is seasonal, most of it occurring in a single month, even in a two-

Fishing boats crowd the harbor in Petersburg, in southeastern Alaska.

week period in some areas. The shellfish industry is much less seasonal.

Except for April and May when the crab molt and spawn, crab may be taken all year. The huge, delicious king crab has become extremely popular. The 1979 landing was second highest in history, and there was a record crop of tanner crab the same year. Shrimp landings, however, declined almost 50 percent from 1978 to 1979.

The forestry industry was almost nonexistent in Alaska until the 1950s, but by 1978 it produced $225 million worth of products. There are two distinct forest ecosystems: the coastal rain forest and the interior forest. The interior forest covers a vast 106 million acres, but its remoteness from markets and land management policies has limited the commercial industry there. The bulk of commercial timber comes from the coastal rain forests, which

The pulp mill at Ketchikan.

The famous Juneau Ice Fields are a dazzling sight on a sunny day.

extend from Cook Inlet to the Alaska-Canada border south of Ketchikan. There is a large pulp mill at Ketchikan that has been operating since 1954, and one in Sitka was completed in 1960. Tree harvesting is done according to good forestry and conservation principles. Ninety percent of all Alaskan wood products are sold to Japan. However, in 1981, Alaska's timber industry dropped to what could be the worst down-cycle in the forest products industry's history. The slump could be due to the world's depressed market for lumber and pulp and has resulted in a 16 percent drop in statewide employment and a 50 percent reduction in logging activity in southeastern Alaska.

A fast-increasing boost to Alaska's economy is the tourist trade. Each year in greater numbers, travelers flock to the state by car along the Alaska Highway, by leisure boat through the Inside

Passage, but most of all by air. Since the 1960s national affluence has shrunk the economic distance that once made Alaska so remote. Thanks to excellent connections, a Texan or New Yorker, with a two-week vacation, can travel north of the Arctic Circle, view the midnight sun, photograph totem poles or the tallest mountain in North America, or set foot on a startlingly beautiful glacier in southern Alaska. Since the early 1970s a large number of Japanese tourists has visited Alaska. The total number of tourists to visit the state in 1981 was approximately 660,000. The tourist industry provides a vast number of jobs, especially for unskilled workers. The main tourist season is June through August.

Gold mining, once Alaska's foremost industry, has declined

The Chilkat Indian dancers from Port Chilkoot are part of the current revival of native arts and crafts.

steadily since the 1940s when gold prices were fixed. Crude petroleum leads all mineral products with natural gas, often found in conjunction with oil, coming third. Second place goes to sand and gravel production, which rose spectacularly during the reconstruction that followed an earthquake in 1964 and remains important for highway and airport construction.

Farming is an industry in the fertile Matanuska and Tanana valleys, but there is stiff competition from foodstuffs flown in from outside. The brief spring and summer is suitable for agriculture thanks to long hours of sunlight. Except for the steady Pribilof Island yield, fur production and fur farming have, like gold, faded to ghosts of their former importance.

The colorful whaling industry used to be important in Alaska and was revived after the Civil War. The two chief uses for whalebone then were to stiffen women's corsets and to make buggy whips. Tailors used it also to make men's shoulders appear broader and squarer than they actually were.

In summer whaling ships used to sail through Bering Strait and east along the north coast of Alaska. The first vessels wintered in 1889 at Herschel Island, just west of the Mackenzie River delta, in what was supposed to be U.S. territory but was later determined to be Canadian. Many whales were captured north of Bering Sea and the Alaskan mainland.

Ships used to winter two or three times on a voyage. The crew usually numbered 49 because law required any ship carrying 50 or more men to have a doctor aboard, and the owners were eager to avoid this expense. The largest whales gave 2,000 pounds of bone, which, at $4 per pound, netted $8,000. The record catch on a single voyage was 69 whales, the average whale giving perhaps 1,000 pounds of bone. The profits were impressive for some—but not for the men before the mast. They worked for a percentage, sometimes as low as 1/200th share of the profit, and easily managed to spend their earnings on what the skipper sold them from the slop chest. These percentages were called "lays." Those of the crew members were very small; the captain's very large, sometimes enabling him eventually to buy his own ship; and the lion's share went to the owners.

This romantic and, for the owner, lucrative business came to a sudden close around 1906. That year more than a dozen ships had wintered at Herschel Island, or points east; thereafter no more than two or three ships wintered, and these devoted themselves almost wholly to trading.

The failure of the whalebone industry was caused by three things that happened simultaneously. Women stopped wearing heavily-boned corsets, men stopped using buggy whips because the automobile was coming in, and somebody invented a substitute called "featherbone." Whalebone dropped in price

Eskimos still hunt whales for food at Point Hope. Here they have harpooned one.

from $4 or $5 per pound to 15 or 20 cents and, indeed, was difficult to sell at any price except in very small quantities.

While commercial whaling died out in Alaska, Eskimo whaling continued, as it had for centuries before the white men took it up. Commercial whalers usually had taken only the whalebone, or black baleen, wastefully discarding the rest of the huge mammals. But to the Eskimo, whale meat is food, and even one or two whales caught per season might spell the difference for an entire village between a year of plenty and a year of want. They love its nourishing meat and consider the skin, with an inch-thick layer of

Muktuk *is a food delicacy to sea-mammal–hunting Eskimos.*

blubber attached, a special delicacy. It is called *muktuk*, or *maktak*, and it is eaten raw. In the areas of Point Hope, Wainwright, and Point Barrow, the Eskimo umiaks are still brought out in the early spring each year for repairs, and a period of great excitement and entertainment for the villagers is begun. Boats are fitted, gear is readied, and the umiaks take to the open waters. Luck and the weather will decide whether many or no whales will be taken. The outcome is of vital concern to the villagers. But just as important as food is the appeal of whaling itself as the hunters confront its dangers, accept its challenges, and display, both individually and in groups, their remarkable seamanship and skill.

John Bockstoce, curator of ethnology at the famous New Bedford Whaling Museum in Massachusetts, is a diligent student of almost every aspect of Alaskan Eskimo whaling: historical, commercial, anthropological, archeological, and practical. For almost a decade he has spent almost half of each year participating in whale hunts originating in Point Hope, Barrow, St. Lawrence Island, and other places. The following is based on information he has generously supplied.

Bockstoce thinks it was the Eskimo invention of the toggle-headed harpoon and the sealskin drag float that enabled the Eskimos to be successful whalers. The air-filled, air-tight sealskin float is attached to the whale by harpoon and retards its movements. As many as a dozen floats can be attached to a single whale, tiring the behemoth each time he dives or swims. The floats "did the hard work and took the punishment," eliminating the dangerous direct battle between whale and crew.

Bockstoce estimates that commercial whalers killed more than 20,000 bowhead whales between the late eighteenth and early twentieth centuries. When they stopped hunting there were fewer than 3,000 left. Only Eskimos sought the bowhead thereafter and between 1920 and 1960 about 50 whaling crews took between 10 and 15 animals a year. The high cost of outfitting a whaling crew kept the number down. Between the oil boom and the building of the pipeline, in the 1970s it suddenly became possible for an ambitious and hardworking Eskimo to earn the $9,000 necessary to outfit a crew and become a whaling captain. By 1976 the catch had increased to 48, with 43 known to have been wounded and gotten away.

The following year, fearing extinction of the species, the International Whaling Commission (IWC) rescinded the Eskimo exception from the total ban on bowhead whaling that had been in force since 1931. The ban came as a shock to the Eskimos. They felt their ancient hunting rights were being denied. In villages where whale meat was a relied-on staple, starvation and death was a possibility. Belatedly the government held hearings where Eskimos explained that it was not only food needs that were at stake. The whale hunt is an important cultural event for Eskimos, a source of pride, a holiday festival, a connection with their past.

An Alaska Eskimo Whaling Commission (AEWC) was formed in 1977 and initiated legal action against the restriction. The government proposed a quota of 15 whales caught or 30 struck, whichever came first. The IWC said no and proposed a limit of 12 caught or 18 struck. The Eskimos felt this was not enough for their nutritional needs, but they wanted to demonstrate their ability to regulate themselves and their strong desire to participate in forming new regulations. With the single exception of one whale at Barrow they managed to stay within the limit. The

IWC expressed sympathy for the Eskimos and increased the quota to 18 whales caught or 27 struck for the next year. From the Eskimo point of view it is ironic that the white man, who was responsible for taking 20,000 whales, should lay down rules for subsistence hunting that Eskimos are expected to obey. Understandably, there is a growing wave of Eskimo sentiment for ignoring IWC quotas and accepting the AEWC's contention that 48 whales are a safe and desirable number to harvest each year. Here is one more issue creating tension between the formerly friendly Eskimos and the increasing number of whites invading their country and presenting them with laws about which they have not been consulted. It adds fuel to the increasing native resentment and militancy.

V / CAPITALS OLD AND NEW

WHO WAS RESPONSIBLE for our purchase of Alaska? Most historians credit William Henry Seward, our secretary of state under Lincoln. Seward reasoned that in order to properly defend the United States we needed Alaska to dominate the North Pacific, and Greenland and Iceland to dominate the North Atlantic. He advocated that we buy Greenland and Iceland from Denmark, and Alaska from Russia, but he succeeded only with the Russian part of his plan. Negotiations were opened with Russia for the purchase of Alaska, a price of $7.2 million agreed upon, and at 4:00 A.M., March 30, 1867, the Treaty of Purchase was signed by Secretary Seward, acting for us, and by Baron de Stoeckl, acting for Russia.

At the time of the purchase the capital of Russian America, as it was called then, was Sitka. To this day it remains the most Russian city in the state. Everywhere in Sitka there are reminders that it was once a thriving imperial metropolis with a gay social life; indeed, it was a cultural center for the entire northwest coast. This city, which all Sitkans, and many non-Sitkans, consider the most picturesque in Alaska, was founded in 1799 when a Siberian trader, Alexander Baranof, moved there from Kodiak Island, site of the first Russian settlement. He arrived with 30 Russians, several hundred Aleuts, and a charter from the Russian America Company, which gave him exclusive rights to all profits that might be derived from any resource whatsoever in the Russian

The old Russian capital is considered the most picturesque city in the state, especially by its loyal inhabitants.

colony. Baranof was under orders to stop the trade in furs and ivory being carried on by other nations. He was also to protect the Indians' lives and property, to feed them in time of disaster, to educate their children, and, if possible, save their souls.

The Indians, unaware of this intended kindness, resisted the newcomers vigorously. Ten of the 30 Russians had constantly to stand on guard. The local people would capture and kill any single man or small group of Russians. In 1802, when Baranof was away visiting Kodiak Island, the Indians captured the post, killing all the men and taking the women and children prisoners. Baranof returned in 1804 and rebuilt the village, naming it New Archangel. The Tlingit Indian word, Sitka, which means the "best place," had long been in use, however, and the new name did not stick.

Hostility between the Indians and the whites continued until as late as 1855, when a battle resulted in a score of deaths and the wounding of 21 Russians and 60 Indians.

At the end of the eighteenth century, when San Francisco was still a mission, Sitka became the largest settlement on the entire Pacific Coast, a center of trade and civilization. Into the exquisite Bay of Sitka, peppered with tiny spruce-covered islets and dominated by towering Mount Edgecumbe, came clipper ships from New England stopping off on their way to China, English

The old Russian Orthodox Church in Juneau.

trading ships, ships from Kronstadt on the Baltic, Spanish ships, and French ships. Here Yankee traders matched wits with Tlingit Indians, the Yankees frequently getting the worst of the bargain. It was the most brilliant city of a huge wilderness empire.

On October 18, 1867, Sitka witnessed the dramatic formal ceremonies that transferred possession of Alaska from Russia to the United States. Russian soldiers in dark red-trimmed uniforms and U.S. troops in full dress stood at attention in front of the governor's castle, making a brave show despite the rain. The Commissioner of the Imperial Ruler of all the Russias said the necessary words and the U.S. commissioner received the land for its new owners. The Russian flag was lowered and the American flag raised in its place, to the accompaniment of tears from the Russian ladies and salutes from the batteries and ships' guns in the harbor. Later most of the Russian families returned to Russia; only a few remained, and their descendants still live in Sitka.

Reminders of Sitka's Russian past turn up at Easter time, when decorated eggs are traded and *kulich*, a sweet holiday bread, is eaten. Two Christmases are celebrated, one at the usual time, the other according to the Russian calendar. Another reason for the

Mt. Edgecumbe outlines the horizon at Sitka.

Sheldon Jackson College was founded in 1878.

continuation of some old Russian customs is that Sitka remains the spiritual center of the Russian Orthodox Church in Alaska.

Saint Michael's Cathedral, which housed many rare icons and souvenirs of old Russian America, was destroyed by fire in 1966. Fortunately, the artistic and historical treasures were saved from the fire. An exact copy of the cathedral was built on the same site from the original plans, a fireproof replica of the Russian original.

Today Sitka is a modern town with a population of 7,803, more than double that of ten years ago. It is famous for its beauty and pleasantly mild climate. Unless flying into the city, you approach it from the sea through a beautiful narrow channel that runs between the shore and Japonski Island. Here you see for the first time the peak of Mount Edgecumbe, an extinct volcano often compared to Fujiyama. The innumerable little green islands that surround the old capital offer calm lagoons for sailing or sheltered landing places for pontoon planes.

The famous Sheldon Jackson school and college, founded in 1878 and the oldest Alaskan school in continuous operation, is at Sitka. Its splendid museum contains interesting Eskimo and

Totems guard the entrance to Sitka National Monument Park.

Indian exhibits collected by Sheldon Jackson early enough to include many rare and unique specimens. The mask collection is particularly wonderful and rich. Many important native leaders attended the school because, until the last decade, there were virtually no high schools outside of the two big cities in Alaska, Fairbanks and Anchorage.

Sitka has hotels, a fine government hospital, a library, a cold storage plant, and the famous Pioneers Home for aged sourdoughs, or old-timers, built on the old Russian parade ground. A pulp mill financed with Japanese capital employs about 400 people full-time. It brought some ten Japanese families to Sitka, which turned out to be interesting for both Sitkans and the newcomers.

The Mount Edgecumbe Boarding School, run by the Bureau of Indian Affairs, is a high school for boys and girls. The high cost of operating this facility, nearly $20,000 per student, may be one of the reasons the bureau is not including it in its proposed budget for 1984.

Sitka houses a splendid collection of totem poles. Eighteen in number, they were gathered from many parts of Alaska for an exhibit in the 1904 Saint Louis Exposition. When the fair was over, Alaska's Governor John Brady succeeded in having them returned to Alaska and placed in Indian River Park, which is now Sitka National Monument Park.

After the purchase, Sitka remained the capital of Alaska until 1900, when the rapidly growing city of Juneau was named as the new seat of government. Governor Brady and the executive offices remained in Sitka until 1906; thereafter the new governor took up his duties in Juneau.

Juneau is still the capital. It stands on Gastineau Channel at the water's edge, framed by the steep, timbered slopes of Mount Juneau and Mount Roberts, which tower above the city. There is so little space between the mountains' edge and the water that one wonders how a town came to be built on this particular spot. The answer is easily found—gold. Juneau's history, like that of other places in the state, begins with the discovery of the yellow metal. Two prospectors, Harris and Juneau, found gold at Silver Bow Basin in 1880, and before the next spring arrived, more than 100 men were camped at the site. This was the first gold rush on Alaskan soil. Harris and Juneau disagreed for two years about naming their camp, and finally a town meeting of miners was held so that a decision might be reached. A compromise was effected by calling the town Juneau and the district Harrisburg.

From the time of the U.S. purchase until 1897 there was a black period of lawlessness in Alaska's history. With no civil law or administration for maintaining order, murder, burglary, and drunkenness were the order of the day. The gold stampeders in the late 1890s and 1900s, although without civil authority, created their own form of local self-government, on the order of New England town meetings. Together with such sporadic administration as was possible through the army, navy, and custom service, this served until 1912, when the Alaskan legislature was created. A modern-thinking legislature it was, too, for in 1913 one of its first acts gave the territory's female citizens the right to vote, a provision not granted to females in the lower 48 until the U.S. constitution was amended in 1920.

Gold mining continued to be the chief industry in Juneau for more than half a century until, in the 1940s when the price of gold was fixed by the federal government and mining costs rose steadily, it no longer paid. The huge Alaska Juneau Mine, once the largest gold-mining operation in the world, reckoning by tonnage, stands silent and empty today. It once employed almost 1,000 men and had an annual payroll of more than a million dollars.

Juneau is connected only by water and air to other cities in Alaska, except for Douglas. Douglas is her twin city; it stands on a wooded island across a narrow channel spanned by a bridge, and since 1971 it has been part of the borough of Juneau.

Alaska's capital city is a modern town of 19,528 people, with tall buildings set on steep hills, reminding one of San Francisco in feeling if not in size. Administrative offices of the federal government are housed in a new many-storied building, and there

Juneau has the most spectacular site of any Alaskan city.

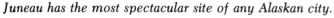

Juneau's links with the rest of Alaska and the world are by air and water.

is a fascinating, handsome, modern Alaskan state museum. Juneau has one of the 12 community colleges that are part of the University of Alaska complex. It is a ferry stop on the Alaska Marine Highway System. The favorite gathering place for legislators, visitors, and townfolk is still the coffee shop of the Baranof Hotel, where issues are hotly debated and many social and business matters settled.

There is a splendid harbor at Juneau, crowded in season by salmon and halibut fishing vessels, which has excellent docking facilities. The capital has a modern airport, with a connecting automobile road running through another of Alaska's startling landscapes. Here are spectacular mountains, brilliant glaciers glistening in the sun, set against dark green, tree-covered slopes, all contributing to a colorful scene of splendor. Nearby Mendenhall Glacier, one of the few in the world accessible by road, is a 17-mile-long ice stream that provides an important tourist attraction, but is also enjoyed and thoroughly explored by native Juneauites. On a sunny day its crevasses reflect the strong blues of sky and surrounding water. Picnicking within sight of it is a local tradition. In Auk Lake outside Juneau you may swim comfortably in summer within sight of a white glacier!

ABOVE: *In summertime Juneauites may swim in surroundings of incomparable beauty.*

LEFT: *Auk Lake with Mendenhall Glacier in the background.*

For almost a quarter of a century Alaskans have debated a burning question. Should their state capital be moved from Juneau and, if so, where? Juneau, reachable only by sea and air, is 600 miles and two time zones from the state's major population areas of Anchorage and Fairbanks. Many Alaskans regard Juneau as an outpost in "Southeastern," only an appendage of the state. At the same time, Anchorage has become the state's commercial center and is roughly half of political Alaska.

The idea of a new capital city largely originated with Robert

Atwood, publisher of the *Anchorage Times*, who wrote a series of columns strongly advocating it. However, citizen initiatives to do this were defeated when they were placed on the state ballot in 1960 and 1962. Frank Harris, the owner of an Anchorage dry-cleaning establishment, took up the idea again after serving as a state senator in Juneau from 1966 to 1968 and finding living conditions in the capital city disappointing. While in the state senate, Harris had been unsuccessful in getting legislation passed to move the capital. He then proceeded to organize a group of volunteer workers who collected signatures for another petition and raised money for the new effort.

A third initiative was finally placed on the state ballot in 1974 and adopted by a majority of Alaskans. Between 1962 and 1974, the population of the Anchorage area had doubled to at last outvote those in the rest of the state who opposed the move from Juneau. The question of where the new capital would be located was yet to be determined.

Under the terms of the successful initiative, the governor appointed a nine-person Capital Site Selection Committee. Most of the members, like the governor, had been opposed to the move. One million dollars was provided for the selection committee to narrow the choice of possible sites. Interestingly, because of the historically intense rivalry between Anchorage and Fairbanks, the initiative excluded both from consideration as the new capital. It also required that any new site possess 100 square miles of land near a road and railroad, which either belonged to the state or was available to it without cost. Such land had to be below 2,000 feet of elevation and appropriate for an airport. Good soil, ample water, appealing topography, and modest annual snowfall were additional search criteria for the committee, which also sought to avoid disturbing the wildlife in the site area.

As a result of the search committee's work, three possible sites for the new capital were placed on the 1976 ballot for a decision by the citizens. Willow, a hamlet of 300 people, approximately 35 miles northeast of Anchorage, won over Larson Lake, near Talkeetna, and Mount Yenlo. Nine months after the voters made their choice, Governor Hammond appointed a nine-member Capital Site Planning Commission to come up with a design plan for a new capital city on the Willow site and to advise the state how it would be developed. The state legislature insisted that the commission plan for a city of no fewer than 30,000 people.

The commission hired as its executive director Morton Hoppenfield, chief planner of Columbia, Maryland, the most successful new town of any size in the lower 48 states. In December 1977, the low-key, distinctly non-monumental design of two small San Francisco firms, Bull, Feld, Volkmann, and Stockwell, architects, and Sedway-Cooke, planners, was selected, and money was provided for them to develop a finished city plan. The architects had been warned that many Alaskans had come there because they disliked the high densities, congestion, and dominance of advanced technology elsewhere and did not want their new home state to acquire those same characteristics. The winning design features structures that define a very approachable, human-scale place—"a city for a client who doesn't like cities." Steep mountain cabin roof lines, church steeples, a great variety of storefronts and elevations, arcaded sidewalks, and canopied street bridges are tastefully combined. Land is also provided for those who would build their own houses. The distant prospect of Mt. McKinley was allowed to rule the overall design, and everything was done to give it maximum exposure to the city. The designers foresaw that a big problem would be attracting people other than those associated with the state government to move there.

With most statewide politicians still opposed to the move of the capital, there continues to be a strong demand for a realistic estimate of its cost. At the time of the 1974 vote, there was an understanding that the move would be carried out by 1988 at a cost of $110 million. A 1978 initiative requires a public vote on the capital transfer costs that are to be paid for by bond issues. That same year, Alaskans turned down a bond proposal for $966 million to begin the project. To date, state officials have been unable to resolve the conflict between the 1974 voter decision to move the capital and the 1978 requirement for public approval of its cost, more recently estimated at $4.4 billion. That conflict deepened when, in the November 1982 elections, Alaskans voted down a $2.8 billion bond issue that would have provided funds to, at least, begin the move. While some believe the increasing cost estimates have caused Alaskans to change their minds about the entire move, others argue that the state's annual $6 billion revenue from North Slope oil makes the move affordable. Meanwhile, Willow remains largely a dream city in the wilderness.

VI / INTERESTING ISLANDS

Looking into Tomorrow

U P NORTH where the Bering and Arctic seas meet and Siberia and Alaska seem to be reaching out to join hands are two rocky little islands, the Diomedes. Standing on Little Diomede you can see across to another hemisphere, into another day of the week! Little Diomede is part of Alaska in the Western Hemisphere, while Big Diomede belongs to the Soviet Union in the Eastern Hemisphere. Only a narrow strait separates the islands, but through this strait runs the International Date Line, on the other side of which is a new day. When it is Monday in Alaska on Little Diomede, it is Tuesday in Siberia on Big Diomede. You can look into tomorrow from Little Diomede or, if you are standing on the larger island, you can peer into yesterday.

The Eskimos who lived on the islands were once related and, with little thought of date lines and international boundaries, used to visit back and forth by boat in summer, or afoot in winter when the strait was frozen over. This was a privilege reserved for Eskimos only, and during World War II this informal and friendly interchange ended. After the war, in 1948, when 18 Little Diomeders thought it time to resume the old ways, they went across to the bigger island to visit and trade as they had often done in prewar times. They were arrested by Soviet officers, imprisoned, but eventually released. Now it doesn't matter whether you are Eskimo or not, it is inadvisable to set foot on Big

115

Diomede. The following year, 1949, the Soviet government moved all the Big Diomede Eskimos to the mainland.

Vitus Bering was a Dane who began his long service in the Russian Imperial Navy at the age of 23. Peter the Great placed him at the head of an expedition charged with determining whether or not the continents of Asia and America were connected. In 1725 he embarked on what has been called one of the most remarkable undertakings in the history of exploration and science—really a series of expeditions, lasting many years and

This village with its cobbled streets on Little Diomede is within sight of Asia.

involving hundreds of men. On August 16, 1728, Saint Diomede's day, he sighted two islands and named them after the saint. A heavy curtain of fog prevented Bering from seeing what he had traveled so far to discover, the coast of America, and he turned back soon afterward. What a trick of fate this was! Had the weather been good he would have returned to Saint Petersburg triumphant. Instead, his first three years of intense labor were considered wasted and the opening expedition of the series counted a failure.

It is a common belief that once there was a land bridge between

Alaska and Siberia by which the animals of North America and Asia migrated back and forth. The Diomedes, placed where the distance between the two continents is smallest, only 56 miles, were probably part of this bridge. Some believe that 20,000, 30,000, or 40,000 years ago, when man first arrived in America from Asia, he was able to walk across Bering Strait on an ice bridge that was part of the glacial age. Others think a land bridge existed then. More likely the first human discoverers of America came in skin boats similar to the Eskimo umiak, which we know is capable of long sea voyages and of carrying 60 or more people. Neither of the Diomedes has a harbor, but that would not have mattered, for skin boats of the day would have been as easy to haul up on a rocky shore as the boats the islanders use today.

The design of an umiak is considered an ancient one and is thought to have changed very little. The umiaks still in use on Little Diomede today have the same sleek lines of their ancestors, but ribs, instead of being made of laboriously spliced driftwood, are now made of imported hardwood and steam bent. Now too, likely as not, there is an outboard motor attached to the stern.

Seal oil may still be used for heating and cooking on Little Diomede Island, but it is burned in an enamel pan instead of a soapstone lamp as formerly, and the wick is made of canvas instead of pussy willow fuzz or moss. Where hunting large game animals is still the chief means of support, fur clothing will be found too, for it is lighter, more comfortable, and more effective against the cold than white man's dress. But the furs are supplemented by cotton dresses worn indoors by the women and cotton parkas worn over the furs to keep them dry. A common sight throughout Eskimo villages in Alaska now is a mixture of the two types of clothing.

Both of the treeless Diomedes rise from beachless shores, with almost perpendicular sides. On the smaller island the houses of the only settlement are perched in terraces along the steep sides of the island. In 1980, 139 people lived in the village, which at first glance resembles a medieval town. It has streets paved with cobblestones, complete with gutters for draining the water.

Unlike most primitive Alaskan Eskimo earth dwellings, the Diomede houses are mainly built of rocks held together with clay. Bits of driftwood are utilized whenever they can be found, supplemented in recent years by imported timber. Roofs were formerly of walrus skin, but shingled roofs are not uncommon now.

The deep surrounding waters supply walrus, still the mainstay of the Diomede diet, but also whale and seal. A few bears and foxes are taken too, but food supplies are supplemented by store-bought canned milk, tea, sugar, flour, cigarettes. Sea ice, which loses its salt content with age, supplies the only water.

In the summertime residents, driven like so many other Eskimos by a need for money to purchase gasoline, sugar, flour, and outboard motors, cross in their skin-covered umiaks to the mainland to earn what they can. The Diomede Islanders, with their wealth of walrus tusk ivory, are excellent carvers, and their cribbage boards and figurines bring high prices in Anchorage and Nome. But the life struggle is harder now than it was before the coming of the white man. Thanks to their isolation, the islanders retained old ways longer than their mainland cousins. "Civilization" has, alas, caught up with them, too. They are now typical in that they are dependent on white men's goods and need to earn the cash money with which to buy them.

Misty Home of the Fur Seals

Two hundred and fourteen miles north of the nearest land are five islands that make up the Pribilof group, also known as the Seal Islands. They are Saint Paul, Saint George, and three much smaller uninhabited islands, Otter, Walrus, and Sealion Rock. The seals arriving here each year are probably the only aquatic animals in the world that have the honor of being escorted to their summer home by the U.S. Coast Guard, which protects them from being illegally hunted at sea.

The islands are named after their Russian discoverer, Gavriil

Group of fur seals, Pribilof Islands.

Pribilof. In 1786, while sailing among the Aleutians, he noticed the migrating seals and decided to try and follow them to their breeding grounds, the location of which had long been a tantalizing mystery. He sailed northward and by chance took an almost direct route to the rookeries. He landed on June 12 and named the new island Saint George, after his ship. So foggy is this area that it was a year before Saint Paul, the larger island, was sighted, although it is only 40 miles away.

Since then the misty Pribilofs have become famous as the largest fur seal rookery and the greatest single source of furs in the world. The precipitous islands are volcanic in origin and for nine days out of ten in summer are enveloped in fog. Here there are only two seasons, foggy wet summer and dry windy winter. The damp summer climate and the numerous sheltered rocky areas are so perfectly suited, however, to the needs of the breeding fur seal that nearly 1.5 million northern fur seals return to these islands each year to mate and have their young. The Pribilof seal differs from fur seals living in the Southern Hemisphere and is unlike the much more widely distributed, smaller, hair seal. The latter animal has a short, stiff-haired pelt, in contrast to the fur seal's silky, luxurious coat, and is hunted for food and fuel by Eskimos from Siberia all the way to Greenland.

Neither of the two larger Pribilofs has a harbor, and navigation is dangerous. The group lies near the southern limit of scattered ice in Bering Sea, and detached pieces of arctic pack may be seen bobbing offshore between February and May. The steep coasts also provide excellent seasonal housing for 100 species of bird life including auklets, cormorants, gulls, murres, kittiwakes, and sea parrots. These bird colonies attract 900 to 1,000 tourists to St. Paul from June through August. Visitors stay at the comfortable hotel owned by Tanadgusix Corporation, St. Paul's Aleut corporation.

Once Pribilof discovered the breeding grounds of the fur seal, wholesale slaughter followed. It has been estimated that between 1799 and 1834 two million animals were killed. From 1835 until the Alaska Purchase, it was forbidden to kill female seals, with a hope of preserving the diminishing herds.

Later, when the route of the annual migration was discovered, came pelagic sealing, the taking of seals at sea. Schooners would follow the herds from the Oregon coast to the Seal Islands, killing as they sailed. They would lie off the islands waiting for the mothers as they went to sea to secure food for their young. This was double murder. If a mother didn't return, her baby died of starvation, since a seal will nurse no pup but her own. In an effort to stop this wanton slaughter the United States called conferences and passed laws, but to no avail. The laws drove the sealers to register under foreign flags, and they managed to get many seals despite patrolling revenue cutters.

By 1910 it was estimated that indiscriminate hunting had reduced the fur seal population from three million to 300,000. In that year our government took charge of the rookeries and finally negotiated a treaty with Great Britain, Japan, and Russia, by which pelagic sealing was outlawed. Since then, through care and scientific management, the herd has increased and in 1981 numbered 1.5 million, an optimum number. Each year a small percentage of young males between three and four years of age are killed for their pelts. The skins are sold at fur auction and then made up into the familiar, long-wearing coats. The 1981 harvest, which took place during the four-week season in July, was about 25,000. For a time in the late 1950s, because of too great an increase in the herd, some females were taken, but that practice has been discontinued. The value of the skins, which has been steadily declining, was $1 million in 1981.

In 1940 Japan denounced the fur seal treaty and proclaimed that her sealers would take animals wherever and whenever they could. In 1957 an interim North Pacific treaty was agreed to by Canada, Japan, the Soviet Union, and the United States. Called the Convention on Conservation of North Pacific Fur Seals, it arranged a sharing of the annual harvests in Alaska and the Soviet Union. Canada and Japan now receive 30 percent of the sealskins; the remaining 70 percent is divided equally between the U.S. and the Soviet Union. Renewed several times, it was extended for four more years by unanimous Senate vote in 1981. At renewal time the Friends of Animals and the Humane Society usually lobby against the convention on the grounds that the killing methods are inhumane. But federal statute decrees that only government employees may do the killing and always in the presence of a humane observer. The Tanadgusix Village Corporation successfully opposed the societies and saved the hunt.

An amendment to the treaty calls for investigating opportunities for the 80 percent of the Pribilof Island residents who are unemployed. Approximately 150 islanders are federal employees. A plant built by federal agents years ago to render the seal oil has been converted to one where the animals, after being skinned, are frozen and sold to a Korean company and crab boat operators for use as bait.

Names given to members of a fur seal family are curious. The mature male is called a "bull," his wife a "cow," and their youngsters are "pups." A bull and his wives constitute a "harem," and a congregation of harems is a "rookery." The three-year-old males are called "bachelors," and they are the ones that are killed each year.

Fur seals are first cousins to the sea lion. They live from 12 to 15 years, and the male usually weighs four to six times as much as the female. After she is three years old the cow gives birth to one pup annually, soon after her arrival on the island. When the pup is weaned, mother goes to sea in search of food for her offspring and may travel great distances, remaining away for days. On her return, by a secret process known only to mother seals, she can always spot her own pup among the thousands of pups waiting on the beach.

Although the Pribilofs are treeless, they are covered in summertime with deep green and yellow-green vegetation, brightened with the color of flowering plants. There are Aleut villages on Saint Paul and Saint George. It was from these settlements, as well as from the Aleutian Islands, that puzzled and dismayed natives were evacuated to Admiralty Island during World War II. They have since returned and today number about 700. Most of them are engaged in the fur seal industry, under the supervision of the National Marine Fisheries Service, Department of Commerce.

Musk-Ox and Reindeer

In clear weather Nunivak Island, the second largest in the Bering Sea, is visible in all directions for about 30 miles. Because it is surrounded by shoals that make boat approaches extremely dangerous, explorers and traders alike gave it a wide berth for many years. This permitted Nunivak's Eskimos to retain their ancient ways longer than their mainland cousins. As late as 1926 Nunivak Islanders still wore bead and walrus ivory labrets, or lip ornaments, discarded long before by other western Eskimos. They still adhered religiously to elaborate ceremonies relating to seal hunting and social life in general. Then, as now, walrus, seal, and fish were plentiful round the island and the Nunivakers were prosperous.

Although the shift from old to new ways came late to the island, which lies off Alaska's western shore about midway between the Aleutians and Seward Peninsula, it was nevertheless inevitable. With the intrusion of a new culture came the missionary, the schoolteacher, and eventually the bush pilot and his plane-load of parcels from mail-order houses. To the Nunivak Eskimos, the change brought not only a new way of life but also two new animals for their island.

In 1935 and 1936, 31 musk-ox, originally imported from Greenland, were moved from the mainland to Nunivak, which is a national wildlife refuge. When the herd grew to almost 600, with danger of overgrazing the island imminent, about 150 were transported to various parts of the Alaskan mainland by the Alaska Department of Fish and Game. These strange, prehistoric-looking beasts formerly roamed throughout the northern part of North America as far south as Kentucky. In mainland Alaska, probably the last native musk-ox was killed south of Point Barrow around the 1870s. The tough, sturdy animals are perfectly adapted to Arctic life, and defend themselves easily against all northern predatory animals except the grizzly bear. Bears were the reason for moving them to Nunivak, where there were neither

Musk-ox mother and calf.

bears nor wolves. Musk-ox do not fear wolves, for wolves will not attack them unless they come upon a lone old animal or a lost calf.

Contrary to their reputation, musk-ox are seldom aggressors. When alarmed they usually run to the top of the nearest knoll, making a defensive formation with big animals on the outside and calves in the center. They charge singly, usually, each one making a short powerful rush of from 10 to 15 yards, then whirling, running back to the herd, facing about and backing into line. Several polar expeditions have reported musk-ox calves that domesticated themselves and became camp pets.

Close to the skin of a musk-ox is a downy wool of incredible softness called *qiviut* by the Eskimos. The short curly hairs of this underfur are interspersed with longer, stiff hairs, similar in texture to a horse's mane, called overhair or, more often, guard hair. The qiviut is shed every spring, but the guard hairs that protect it remain permanently. Short-legged and thick-bodied as they are, during the shedding season in April or May their legs are often invisible. The shedding wool drags in long tags after the animals, and wisps may be picked up from the ground and bushes. The Eskimos call the musk-ox *umingmak*, the bearded one.

In 1954 John Teal transferred seven musk-ox calves from the Canadian Arctic to his Vermont farm to start the Institute of Northern Agricultural Research, now known popularly as the Musk-Ox Project. A decade later he captured nine males and 24 female calves on Nunivak Island and took them to a farm at the University of Alaska where they increased to over 100. Since 1977 the University of Alaska has not been associated with the project. The musk-ox were relocated on one big farm near Unalakleet under the parent organization of the Institute of Northern Agricultural Research. Musk-ox Producer's Cooperative, called Oomingmak, markets the exquisitely soft qiviut products. John Teal, the president of the former and secretary of the latter organization, died in 1982.

Domestication of the musk-ox was undertaken to provide a source of cash and employment for northern people who didn't want to leave their villages. To pay for food, fuel, and shelter that they can no longer obtain for themselves, many natives must leave their family for a part of each year to earn money. Rather than raise musk-ox for meat, the far more valuable qiviut is the preferred end product, for it is worth approximately $50 a pound. An animal produces between five and a half to seven pounds of wool annually during its 20- to 25-year lifetime.

Qiviut is finer, longer-fibered, and softer than cashmere, and half its weight. It is extremely warm and will not shrink even when washed in hot water. The sale of qiviut products has been a great success despite the high prices; scarves in 1983 sell for between $115 and $125.

Musk-ox cows carry their young for about eight months, and babies weigh about 20 pounds at birth. They are easily tamed and taught to drink milk from a can fitted with a nipple. At six months they are dehorned, which protects them from one another and prevents injury to the herders.

In 1968 a project specialist visited Nunivak Island to conduct the first training class for Eskimo women in knitting with qiviut, which has an attractive pale brown color. Patterns are based on traditional Eskimo motifs, and a new graphic method of stitch notation was invented for knitters speaking little or no English. Today, about 300 tundra/coastal families make a portion of their annual income from the domestic musk-ox industry. This cottage industry enables natives to remain in their small villages working at their own pace in their own homes.

Nunivak's other introduced animal is the reindeer, our name for a wild caribou when it is domesticated. Originally imported from Siberia into Alaska during the nineteenth century to supplement the native's dwindling supply of food, the dark brown, sometimes spotted, animals increased in population rapidly until at their peak they numbered half a million. Through neglect and ignorance they were almost wiped out during the late 1940s. In a few cases reindeer were placed on islands that had no wolves, their chief enemy, and were permitted to run freely. They increased in number sufficiently to tax the grazing facilities of the islands, posing a threat of overgrazing and eventual starvation. Reindeer "moss," properly a lichen, is their main food. It is an extremely slow-growing plant, requiring many years to renew itself.

The Nunivak reindeer, numbering in the thousands today, are all descendants of 99 animals landed on the island by the government in 1920. The Bureau of Indian Affairs erected a reindeer slaughtering plant to take care of the natural increase, for if protected from wolves a herd will double in three years. The meat is used to supplement native diets locally and elsewhere in Alaska. Ownership of the herd has now been turned over to the Nunivak natives.

Baling reindeer skins on Nunivak.

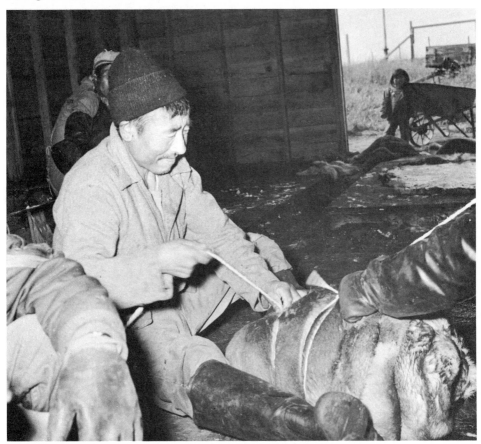

Ugrug *or bearded seal mask from Mekoryuk.*

Reindeer are permitted to wander freely throughout the island all year. At butchering time they are herded, and suitable animals are picked for slaughtering. Reindeer are sensitive and if startled tend to stampede, milling around and around clockwise, in a tightly packed formation. All dogs in the neighborhood are tethered and kept out of sight at this time, because their resemblance to wolves will frighten the reindeer and might start them running.

Eskimo women skin the animals. Flesh and fat are scraped from the skins, which are then hung up outdoors to be dried by wind and sun.

Despite the fashionable invasion of white man's food, thinking, and technology, there are some areas where Eskimo craft is still preserved because it surpasses anything the white man can devise. The skin boat is a good example. Wooden boats are in use on the island, to be sure, but for gliding swiftly and silently through ice-choked waters in search of seal or other game, the light, slender kayak is still supreme. Umiaks, too, still compete successfully with wooden boats on Nunivak, because they are lighter and have a greater carrying capacity for their size. As mentioned before, they require extra care—the skin cover must be dried out between voyages to prevent rotting—but they never require scraping and painting as wooden boats do.

At Mekoryuk, the main settlement on Nunivak, the population dwindled to 161 by 1980. The island is famous for its beautiful ceremonial masks depicting bird or animal images, which may be seen decorating the walls of Alaskan homes as well as museums

Blue onion-shaped domes top the still active Russian Orthodox Church on Kodiak Island.

throughout the world. The masks are still made and sold to visitors or to the Native Arts and Crafts Service, which distributes them to gift shops throughout Alaska.

Shrimp Capital of the World

Kodiak, site of the first Russian colony in Alaska, is in the Gulf of Alaska on northeastern Kodiak Island. Damaged in an earthquake in 1964, it was rebuilt and soon became the largest fishing port in dollar volume in the United States and the largest shrimp port in

Kodiak's Historical Society and Museum is housed in a building dating from the first Russian settlement in Alaska.

Many souvenirs of the Russian-American period of Alaska's history, including icons, furniture, and household goods brought to the New World by Russian settlers, are preserved in Kodiak's museum.

the world. Almost 5,000 people live in Kodiak. Like Sitka, it has many reminders of its Russian past. Russian names are encountered everywhere. The first Russian Orthodox church was built here and is still functioning. Father Herman, who led the first Christian mission to Alaska in 1794, was canonized and became Saint Herman in March 1969 in impressive ceremonies.

The present-day Historical Society and Museum is in a building constructed by Alexander Baranof's men. Since 1966 Frank Brink's "Cry of the Wild Ram," a pageant depicting the early history of Russian Kodiak, is given annually in a beautiful outdoor theater. The entire town is involved in the production, which is a great tourist attraction.

The harbor is crammed with fishing vessels, and many processing plants handle and freeze the shrimp, crab, halibut, and scallops caught in neighboring waters. The navy still maintains a station built in 1940 on Kodiak and it is a stop on the Alaska Marine Highway.

Islands of the Smoky Sea

The treeless Aleutian Islands are the tops of a partially submerged mountain range that once linked Asia and America. Forming a continuation of the Alaska Range, the islands curve westward in a great arc to separate Bering Sea on the north from the Pacific Ocean to the south. From Alaska Peninsula to the outermost end of the chain almost 80 volcanoes have been counted, more than half of which have been active since records began to be kept in the eighteenth century.

A surprising number of people think of these islands as Arctic, but actually they lie between 800 and 1,000 miles south of the Arctic Circle, in the latitude of England and northern France. In addition to innumerable islets and rocks, they consist of 14 large and about 55 small, mountainous islands. The five main groups are the Fox Islands, closest to the mainland, the Islands of the Four Mountains, the Andreanofs, the Rat Islands, and the Near Islands, named for their nearness to Kamchatka but farthest from the rest of Alaska.

The Aleutians are among the foggiest places in the world. When cold air meets warm air, fog is produced. At the Aleutian Islands the icy waters of Bering Sea sideswipe the warm Japan current of the north Pacific Ocean. The result is what aviators call "pea soup" fog.

There are said to be only two seasons here: a rainy, foggy, cool summer, and a comparatively mild, somewhat clearer winter. The thermometer never drops as low as zero, but cold, wet winds of high velocity blow across from Siberia to combine with warm air masses from the south. They produce rain, fog, mist, and snow. Good weather is rare and brief, shifting swiftly as the winds change. "Uncertain" is a word often used to describe Aleutian weather; "terrible" is probably the adjective *most* used.

"Williwaw" ("woolie" to the Yankee whalers of old) is a term familiar to all Aleutian Islanders but known too along other Alaskan coasts. It is a violent puff of wind that sweeps down suddenly with great force from a mountain slope. Because they come without warning and successive gusts change direction unexpectedly, williwaws are dangerous to vessels at sea or in harbor. A boat will toss wildly and is likely to break out her anchor or capsize. A man cannot stand against a strong williwaw, and sailors, particularly those on small sailboats, have a healthy terror of them.

Williwaws, fog, and sudden storms have been responsible for some of the nicknames applied to the Aleutians. Birthplace of the Winds, Islands of the Smoky Sea, and Cradle of the Storms are among the more romantic ones. During World War II many soldiers stationed there invented new ones, few of them romantic and most of them not even polite. A rueful joke that made the rounds was "if the Japanese capture the Aleutians, it will serve them right." The men who had to fly bombing and scouting missions from Aleutian bases had cause for fear and complaint— fog, as well as Japanese gunfire, took many lives.

The innumerable passes between the islands have strong and treacherous tidal currents. Contrary to popular belief, these channels are ice-free throughout the year. Sea ice never forms in the Aleutians except on the inner bays. The ocean is equally free of ice north and south of the chain. If you spent ten years atop the highest of the Aleutians with a telescope looking north into the Bering Sea you would never see a cake of ice. It is only when you travel eastward toward Bristol Bay that floes begin to appear in the north.

The mild, highly intelligent Aleuts who inhabit these islands are of the same racial stock as the Eskimos. Although their languages were once the same long ago, when the people separated, their languages changed in different ways. Now, although related in structure and vocabulary, they differ enough so that people cannot understand one another. Aleut has two distinct dialects, Eastern and Western, the dividing line falling east of Atka Island. It is a dying language; only an estimated 700 Aleuts are able to speak it today. Like the Eskimo, the Aleut is of medium size, with short legs, large head and face, Mongoloid eyes, straight black hair, and a scanty beard. They probably came to the islands from the mainland of Alaska in two separate migration waves. We think the first was more than 4,000 years ago, the second within the last 1,000 years. It is thought that in their heyday they may have numbered 20,000—a far larger number than any neighboring Alaskan areas could support. But the surrounding sea was plentiful in sea lions, seals, and whales, all of which provided food. Salmon and fowl were available, too, and, of great importance, there were ample supplies of driftwood for boat, tool, and weapon building. Aleut culture successfully aimed at developing self-sufficient individuals in a cooperative community. Few genuine Aleuts survive today—estimates vary from one-tenth to one-sixteenth of their original number. Over half of them live outside of the Aleutian Islands now, chiefly in the Pribilofs and on the Soviet Komandorski Islands. Census lists always show a higher figure because they include all native peoples living in the Aleutian area. To further confuse the picture, some Eskimos call themselves Aleuts and some Aleuts call themselves Eskimos. The 1980 census listed 6,500 Aleuts.

The Aleut decline began soon after the Russians found the islands in 1741. Traders followed the explorers and were greeted hospitably by the friendly Aleuts. It is one of the most lamentable stories of European relations with "natives" that the Russians returned kindnesses with cruelties, thefts, and brutal killings, virtually enslaving the entire population. Aleuts were forced to spend their time hunting the fabulous sea otter and, of course, to turn over the skins to the local representative of the Russian America Company. Both the Aleut and the sea otter decreased rapidly thereafter. Umnak Island, one of the Fox Islands, which once sheltered 22 villages and 2,000 people, had by 1980 a single village, Nikolski, with a total of only 50 inhabitants.

The sea otter, which has one of the most precious of all furs, played an important role in early Alaskan history. Single skins

---

An Aleut housewife blowing air through washed seal intestine. It will be stretched, dried, and eventually made into a waterproof coat.

have brought up to $1,500. Four times heavier than the land otter, the sea otter is about four feet long and may weigh anywhere from 30 to 90 pounds. The otters were practically exterminated during the eighteenth and nineteenth centuries by Russian fur hunters, or *promyshlenniki.*

It all started when the members of Vitus Bering's last expedition, sick and dying of scurvy, were shipwrecked on Bering Island. Here they found sea otters in abundance. The fresh meat cured their disease and gave them strength to build from the wreckage of their vessel a tiny namesake, the *Saint Peter.* Its limited cargo space was filled with fresh meat for the voyage back to Siberia, and into the remaining spaces the crew stuffed as many otter skins as they could. When they arrived in Petropavlovsk in 1742 they found the skins fetched enormous prices. In the Chinese market otter skins were the costliest, valued even above sable. This inspired Siberian hunters to extend their hunting operations across Bering Strait to Alaskan waters.

So successful and greedy were the hunters that by the turn of this century the sea otter was thought to be extinct. Around 1910 the U.S. government forbade the taking or sale of these animals, imposing heavy fines for the mere possession of a skin. Slowly a tiny remnant of the once huge herd began to increase.

In 1939 on Amchitka Island, largest of the Rat Island group, an interesting experiment in animal conservation began. As the "pods," or colonies, of sea otters grew, surplus animals were transplanted to other suitable islands to further increase their number. Today they are abundant in Alaskan waters.

Otters are one of the few tool-using animals. The beguiling mammals use a stone to crack the shells of the crab, mussel, abalone, and other shellfish they eat.

While the Russian role in the Aleutians was generally a grisly one, an exception to the rule can be found in the life of Father Ivan Veniaminov. He was not the first Russian missionary of Greek Orthodox faith in the Aleutians, but he was the first to master the difficult Aleut language and to interest himself in Aleut culture and welfare. In a native skin kayak, he paddled from island to island questioning people about their traditions and customs. For a decade following 1824 he lived in Unalaska, preaching and teaching, but also learning. Adapting the old Russian Cyrillic alphabet for the purpose, he created an Aleut alphabet, which greatly aided the people in preserving their wonderfully complicated ancient language. Veniaminov opened a school for Aleut children. He translated the Catechism and the Gospel of Saint Matthew into Aleut and wrote an Aleut grammar. His painstaking writings are still source material for anthropologists and linguists. Under the name of Innocent, Father Veniaminov finally achieved the highest office of his church when he became Metropolitan of Moscow.

Many Russian traders settled in the Aleutians, marrying native women. Modern Aleuts have a large measure of Russian blood; almost all have Russian names. Their church remains the Russian Catholic, or Greek Orthodox, church.

A thrill of horror swept Alaska and the United States when, six months after Pearl Harbor, in June 1942, the battleground of World War II shifted from far places to North America itself. The Japanese bombed Atka and Dutch Harbor, where a U.S. navy base was located. The following day they occupied Attu, the outermost Aleutian Island, killed the schoolteacher who was trying to send out news of the invasion, and took his wife and every other resident of the island prisoner. They were taken to Japan and interned in prisoner-of-war camps, where many of them died. Kiska Island was occupied, too.

Shortly afterward everyone living in the Aleutians was evacuated to the mainland. Forced to leave behind all they owned, the Aleuts were taken to evacuation camps in southeastern Alaska where many of them, for the first time in their lives, saw trees. The only battle of the war on U.S. soil occurred in May 1943, when American infantry, after 19 days of shelling and sniping, recovered Attu from the Japanese.

At the war's end in 1945, Aleuts were permitted to return to their homes—all, that is, except the Attuans. Attu, one of the Near Islands, 1,400 miles west of Anchorage, is a lonely, isolated spot.

An Aleut wedding in the Russian Orthodox Church. The crowns, symbolizing holiness of marriage, must not rest on the couple's heads.

Its buildings had all been demolished in the war. Although the Attuans were eager to go home, the government decided their island should not be reoccupied and that Attuans should live on Atka Island, closer to the mainland and easier to defend. So now Atka, some 500 miles east of Attu, about midway in the chain, has the honor of being the most westerly community in North America—much more westerly than the Hawaiian Islands.

Sailing westward from Alaska Peninsula you would pass Unimak Island, the first of the Aleutian chain, separated from the mainland by narrow Isanotski Strait, or False Pass. This is the largest of the eastern Aleutians, and the home of magnificent Shishaldin Volcano, locally referred to as Smoking Moses. Several times in recent years Shishaldin, which rises majestically for almost 10,000 feet, has been in eruption. Faint wreaths of smoke and vapor still drift from its summit, making a striking picture, for the volcano is largely snow-clad. Pogromni Volcano, whose Russian name means "desolation," is a smaller conical peak, also snow-covered, near the western end of the island.

Akutan Island, one of the Central Fox Islands, was once an important whaling station. Commercial whaling is no longer a local industry, but the Aleut settlement remains.

Unalaska, the next large island, is mountainous, and during the greater part of the year its higher elevations remain snowy. Makushin Volcano, more than 6,000 feet high, forms the peak of the island. Unalaska Bay, on the northern shore and open to Bering Sea, is one of the most important bays in western Alaska. It contains the harbors of Iliuliuk Bay, Unalaska Harbor, and Dutch Harbor.

The port of Unalaska, founded by Solovief in the eighteenth century as a fur trading station, was officially opened as a U.S. customs port during the Klondike gold rush. It had been much used by American and Russian vessels for years before that since it is a good halfway station for ships plying between Seattle and Nome. Dutch Harbor in Unalaska Bay was once a flourishing settlement and the capital of the fur sealing industry.

Atka Island, mentioned earlier, is the largest of the Andreanof group. It contains Korovin Volcano, which rises about 4,000 feet. The island is rugged and volcanic, and smoke still issues occasionally from its northern end. There is a Russian Orthodox church and also a government schoolhouse at the settlement, which had a population of 93 in the 1980 census.

Aleut women on Atka, and on Attu also, were famous for their exquisite baskets made of beach grass, which often took two or more years to complete. Wild rye, which commonly grows on Aleutian beaches to a height of four to five feet, was the grass used for making mats as well as baskets. It was gathered in the fall as it began to turn brown, then split into thin strands and bleached. After this, the long process of weaving began, with the grass stored in something damp to keep it moist and pliable. In more recent times, bits of colored embroidery silk were woven with the grass to produce beautiful designs. The result was a watertight masterpiece, prized by Aleut and white man alike. Most of these old baskets are to be found only in museums or in the collections of a lucky few, but the art is being revived again as part of the renewed interest in native arts and crafts.

In summertime, most able-bodied men on Atka leave the

Unalaska is the largest town in the Aleutians. Note the Russian Orthodox Church to which the Aleuts still belong.

village for the Pribilof Islands where they work in the fur seal rookeries. Their summer earnings are the sole cash income in the village; without it they would have great difficulty getting through the winter.

The rest of the Andreanof Islands are relatively unimportant, but they have strange, musical names like Koniuji, Igitkin, Kanaga, Tanaga, Kavalga, Unalga, Ulak, and Ilak.

Kiska, one of the Rat Islands, has more level ground than most of the islands and is the best harbor in the area. In World War II it was occupied for a time by the Japanese after the attack on Dutch Harbor.

At the end of the chain are the Near Islands, Agattu, and the outermost Attu. Across the International Date Line, the Komandorski Islands, belonging to the Soviet Union, form a continuation of the Aleutian arc, reaching toward Kamchatka and another way of life.

VII / OTHER ALASKAN CITIES

ANCHORAGE IS the largest, richest, most powerful city in Alaska. Surrounded by the magnificent snow-clad Chugach Mountains, it is the big business center of the state. Oil and aviation companies have their main headquarters here, as does the Alaska Railroad, and the city's port is the busiest in Alaska. New office, hotel, and home construction goes on constantly but never seems to catch up with the city's needs. Anchorage, with its surrounding suburbs and villages, is big enough to have luxurious skyscraper hotels, shopping centers, and chain and department stores; thus, unlike most other Alaskan cities, there is a good deal of business competition, which brings down Alaska's notoriously high cost of living slightly. It has radio stations, and four television stations broadcast the three major networks plus National Education Television to its residents. The *Anchorage Daily News*, one of the two competing daily newspapers, won the 1976 Pulitzer Prize for public service. Anchorage has the advantages of a large city combined with easy access to wilderness country for the hunters, fishermen, and nature lovers who want to get away from the daily city grind.

Anchorage's location, slightly north of 61° north latitude, accounts for wide annual variations in length of daylight, which enables one to view a midnight baseball game played in June without lights as well as a winter drive-in movie matinee. The Alaska Range and the Chugach Mountains protect the city from

143

High-rise buildings now interrupt the view of snow-capped mountain peaks in Anchorage.

the bone-numbing temperatures found in Alaska's interior. Constantly moving waters of Cook Inlet also moderate temperatures during the long winters. The inlet has the second greatest tide range in North America with maximum diurnal range during spring tides of 38.9 feet. These extreme tides also produce the bore tide, a steep wall of foaming water. Usually bores are one or two feet high, but spring tides in Turnagain Arm of Cook Inlet can be up to six feet as the tide comes in.

Alaska's first international airport in Anchorage played a pioneer role in the beginning of the Europe-to-Asia Great Circle air route. In November 1956 Scandinavian Airlines inaugurated the first line to fly directly across the geographic North Pole on its Copenhagen-to-Tokyo run. Today every major carrier with routes from the United States to Asia offers at least one flight via Alaska. The largest, most luxurious planes in the world land here now, bringing Europeans and Asians, especially Japanese, to Anchorage. The latter are a familiar sight in many Alaskan cities not only as tourists but as directors and employees of the numerous Japanese-financed enterprises that now exist in the state. Eskimos visiting or working in Anchorage are often difficult to distinguish from the Japanese, which isn't surprising since their physical beginnings thousands of years ago were linked.

In the early 1970s natives in large numbers migrated to Alaska's major cities. Drawn by job opportunities, educational benefits, or perhaps just a spirit of adventure they encountered all the problems accompanying assimilation into a different culture. Naturally friendly and helpful, natives were looked upon strangely in the cities. Coming from villages where everyone's

A major thoroughfare in Alaska's largest city.

standard of living was the same, they never considered themselves poor. In cities the natives found themselves stigmatized as poverty-stricken. However, many found the cities interesting or at least profitable enough to remain. Charles Anderson, an Aleut, began working for the police department when it was unusual for a native to do that. Today, he is Anchorage's chief of police. Natives account for over 10,000 of the inhabitants of Anchorage, giving rise to the remark that it is "the biggest native village of them all." Several of the regional corporations formed under the Alaska Native Claims Settlement Act of 1971 have offices in Anchorage; these multimillion dollar corporations need to be near the financial center of the state to conduct business.

Anchorage has a handsome Historical and Fine Arts Museum, one of the city's major tourist attractions. In addition to its general exhibits, it sponsors an annual Alaska Festival of Native Arts, doing its part to encourage the native culture and craft revival that is taking place throughout Alaska and to raise its artistic level. An experimental Arts and Crafts Center has been established recently in Anchorage to provide help for all native artisans, whether Eskimo, Indian, or Aleut. Training, research opportunities, and advice in marketing and small business development is being offered.

An indication of the resiliency of Anchorage and its 50,000 inhabitants is its recovery from the 1964 earthquake. Worst in Alaskan and North American history, it was the second most severe recorded in the world. In a terrible five minutes $200 million worth of damage was sustained as great gaps opened in the earth. With government aid and its own dynamic spirit, within two years most of the damage was repaired and the city was flourishing once more.

An event of importance to all Alaska occurred just outside Anchorage in the late summer of 1957. An oil strike was made by the Richfield Company close to the city, which started an "oil rush" throughout the Kenai Peninsula. Up to that date every drop of fuel oil burned in Alaska had to be imported, with costly freight charges added to the retail price. Excitement swept the country and crowded other news off the front pages of all newspapers when word of oil "in our backyard" first reached Anchorage. True, the navy some years before had drilled for oil and found it around Umiat and elsewhere in the Point Barrow region, but that had been in a naval reserve area and held no meaning for the average citizen interested in keeping down the cost of his fuel bills. The rest is history, described in Chapter I.

Anchorage is the home of the largest native hospital in the state, Alaska Native Service Hospital, serving the needs of the native community here as well as the rest of the state. In addition, Providence Hospital and the Alaska Hospital serve the medical needs of this thriving city. Providence Hospital completed a large addition in 1976 and now offers a full range of services including open-heart surgery, cobalt treatment, and a frostbite/burn center.

In 1940 the first detachment of U.S. troops arrived in Anchorage to start work on a new air base. Today the huge installations of Fort Richardson and Elmendorf Field have swelled both the temporary and permanent populations, increasing the prosperity of local businessmen as well as the rate of inflation. Anchorage is only one spot, but a central, key one, in a tremendous network of airfield bases that, like the DEW Line, was established in Alaska to maintain U.S. defenses.

Long-distance and even intrastate communications constitute one more of Alaska's problems. White Alice was an early answer. In the late 1970s, RCA began construction on a network of 21 large earth satellites. It already owned a large earth station at Talkeetna. Originally built by Comsat, a commercial satellite company, but sold to RCA, it served the Anchorage area for long-distance and TV communications. Today satellites effectively link Anchorage with the rest of the world.

The Golden Heart of Alaska

The word *gold* has a glamorous sound! It has power, too, enough to lure thousands of hopefuls to Alaska around the turn of this century, and it meant different things to different people. Some who came wanted a fortune, overnight if possible. Some were fleeing the crowded, dirty cities and wanted only untainted air to breathe and lots of space. Many were running from trouble, real or imagined—family, work, or money trouble. For some older men it was the last, lone hope of finding "success." A few women, considered very daring, came too. Idealists, cynics, workers, loafers, adventurers, and writers—they all poured into the territory. There was plenty of room for them in Alaska.

Some lucky few struck gold, but far more eventually gave up prospecting and turned to keeping shops, restaurants, and roadhouses. The fortunate ones who knew a trade, such as carpentry, found it more lucrative in the long run than panning for gold. These "sourdoughs" formed the nucleus of many Alaskan towns, including Fairbanks.

In 1902 Felix Pedro discovered gold on what is now Pedro Creek. By September of the same year enough prospectors had arrived to hold a meeting, appoint a recorder, and name the place "Fairbanks" after their vice-president.

News of the strike spread rapidly, but it was followed by disappointment when the gold-bearing bedrock was found to be buried 80 to 100 feet under muck and gravel, much of it frozen hard in the permafrost. This meant that expensive equipment was needed to extract the gold. It was hard on the lone prospector, but it prevented the kind of mushroom development that nearly or quite wrecked several other gold rush towns.

In many sections around Fairbanks the rich pay dirt was worked out long ago. In the 1950s the most productive gold mining operation in Alaska was that of the U.S. Smelting, Mining and Refining Company outside Fairbanks. Mass production mining undertaken by million-dollar corporations took over the major portion of the industry. Giant gold dredges operating continuously 24 hours a day, creaking and groaning, took chunks of the countryside at a bite, retained the gold ore and discarded the slag, and left behind a strange, useless surrealistic landscape.

Fairbanks is on the Tanana, a branch of the mighty Yukon River, about 120 miles south of the Arctic Circle. Of our big cities, it is the farthest north. Because it is an administrative, transportation, and supply center for the interior and entire North Slope of Alaska, Fairbanks has a commercial importance beyond its size. Often called the "Golden Heart of Alaska," its trade area is estimated at 227,000 square miles. Both the Alaska Railroad and the Alaska Highway terminate at Fairbanks, which had about 22,000 inhabitants in 1980. The Tanana Valley is one of the best farming regions in Alaska, especially for cereals, but full advantage has not yet been taken of its possibilities. Like Anchorage, Fairbanks has an international airport.

The Chena River flows through the center of Fairbanks. In August of 1967 it flooded almost the entire city, producing the worst catastrophe in Fairbanks's history.

The possible hours of sunshine in Fairbanks can vary from four in midwinter to nearly 22 in summer. Being far from the ocean and its climatic influences, Alaska's second largest city is generally both colder in winter and hotter in summer than coastal settlements. During the long summer days, which darken to only a bright twilight around midnight, Fairbanks's temperatures frequently rise to 90° F in the shade—the record is 99°. In winter, as nights grow longer, the cold becomes intense. The thermometer drops to 60° below or lower (the record low is −66°) and the air becomes breathlessly still, for seldom do winds blow at extremely low temperatures, except in the Antarctic. While some activity stops, the railroad continues to run, bringing mail, freight, and passengers; planes arrive and take off—life goes on.

Ice fog, a midwinter phenomenon common to all high Arctic regions, is a real hazard in Fairbanks. It occurs when water vapor mixes with extremely cold air. The water vapor may be naturally produced by animals, people, or industry, and when it meets low temperatures it is frozen into tiny ice crystals. It is similar to fog

The University of Alaska campus from the air.

that occurs elsewhere except that what is water vapor fog in lower latitudes becomes ice fog farther north. In Fairbanks ice fog can persist for a week and even ten days, cutting down visibility and making driving and aircraft landings dangerous. The presence of dust and industrial wastes in the air worsens the situation, and what is a spontaneous occurrence at −40° F occurs now, thanks to pollution, at −20°. Fairbanks is particularly prone to ice fog because it is surrounded by hills on three sides, and there is little wind to disperse the fog. The problem is compounded by temperature inversions when heavy cold air settles in an area and stays. The lower the temperature, the more numerous the frozen particles and the smaller they are, until, like pollen, they simply float in the air and are almost impossible to dislodge. When temperatures fall below −22°, ice fog warnings are issued like storm bulletins. The Geophysical Institute at the university is working on the problem.

The University of Alaska, Fairbanks, opened in 1922, was the first unit of the statewide system of higher education. Since then the system has grown in size to include two more urban university centers at Anchorage and Juneau, as well as 12 community colleges scattered throughout the state. The Fairbanks campus, administrative seat of the entire university system, remains the only residential campus.

As the heart of Alaska's intellectual life and research, by 1980 the University of Alaska, Fairbanks, had expanded to include two colleges and five professional schools, with more than 30 departments offering 140 degrees. That same year it had its highest enrollment, over 3,000 students. This main campus permits an extraordinarily wide range of scholarly pursuits, ranging from the study of scientific stations on floating ice islands in the Polar Sea to courses on the domestication of musk-ox. All the peculiarly northern physical phenomena are present or handily nearby—

The Geophysical Institute at the university houses many internationally-known scientists as well as graduate students.

glaciers, muskeg, permafrost, and aurora borealis—and an extra-
ordinary number of scholars and scientists constantly streams in
and out of the university, summer and winter, as northern science
generally widens its boundaries. Native history, folklore, and
languages are being studied in depth and taught in new ways.
Wildlife, the still relatively unexplored mineral resources, problems of northern agriculture, and the strange uneven quality
of Alaska's economy are all subjects studied by the large number
of departments, institutes, and centers related to the university.
Many federally funded projects work with and through the
university.

One of the liveliest and most impressive places on the Fairbanks campus is the Geophysical Institute, first of the university's
noted research institutes, which opened in 1949. It had the
distinction of being first to spot Sputnik, the Russian space
satellite that led all the rest. The institute is staffed by scientists of
the highest caliber, some of them world famous. There are
laboratories for earthquake prediction, argon gas dating, paleo-
magnetism, and other exotic studies. The students learn by doing
and by assisting their professors. The atmosphere there, as
throughout the university, is easy, informal, and outdoorsy, still
retaining a frontier feeling.

The University of Alaska Museum, which moved to new,
expanded facilities in 1980, was greatly augmented as a result of
the late Dr. Otto W. Geist's expeditions to Saint Lawrence Island.
A pioneer in Alaskan paleontology, Dr. Geist gathered a famous
collection of fossil materials to add to the historical items in the
museum.

Strangely enough the gold-mining companies were the richest
source of fossil skeleton remains of Alaska's prehistoric beasts.
Dredging operations on nearby creeks in and around Fairbanks
turned up quantities of bones from animals that roamed the
country tens of thousands of years ago. It was Dr. Geist who first
realized that this was a "golden" opportunity in a non-metallic
sense. He obtained the cooperation of the U.S. Smelting, Refining
and Mining Company, the American Museum of Natural History,

An automated laboratory at the Geophysical Institute that records seismic activity from various stations. Information gathered is used in earthquake prediction studies.

and the university, to permit him to rescue these important scientific finds. He instructed the mining operators to send for him if any promising bit of ancient bone was revealed as they worked. Geist would dash to the spot, excavate the site carefully, and only then would mining continue. Thanks to the perfect deepfreeze qualities of permafrost, centuries-dead mammoths, some with their flesh and hair intact, have been preserved.

Another area where students gain practical as well as theoretical knowledge at the university is in anthropology. Each summer, field trips are made to study Eskimos and other Indians, often with a professor as leader. Archeological work is sometimes done at the same time or on separate expeditions.

A startling archeological find was made in Alaska in 1939 and 1940 by two faculty members, Froelich G. Rainey and Louis Giddings, and by a visiting Danish Eskimo archeologist, Helge Larsen. At Point Hope, a peninsula in northwestern Alaska that juts into the Polar Sea, they discovered the remains of a unique Arctic metropolis. They unearthed a group of 800 dwellings

On the university campus a radio telescope is shown here silhouetted against an auroral sky.

arranged in regular avenues that must have housed a population larger than that of pre-war Fairbanks! Point Hope is 130 miles north of the Arctic Circle, beyond 68° north latitude.

The site, called Ipiutak, is thought to have been built well over 1,000 years ago. Excavations yielded beautiful ivory carvings, some of them unlike those of any known northern Eskimo or Indian culture. About 500 skeletons were recovered. In strange tombs, fashioned of logs, skeletons were revealed that stared up at the archeologists with artificial eyeballs carved of ivory and inlaid with huge jet pupils. Before burial the natural eyes had apparently been gouged out and replaced with ivory substitutes. Ivory mouth covers and nose plugs carved to represent bird beaks added to the fantastic appearance of the skulls. Exquisite spiral carvings of walrus ivory, of unknown use, and delicately made and engraved implements were found in the burials. Many designs of the artifacts resembled those produced in North China 2,000 or 3,000 years ago; others were like carvings of the Ainu peoples in northern Japan and Amur River natives of Siberia. This was not the culture of a simple people, but of a highly sophisticated, complex group.

Twentieth-century Point Hope, or Tigerak, "the forefinger," as it is known to the Eskimos, supports a population of 461. The question arises as to how such a large settlement as nearby Ipiutak could have been fed. The answer that comes quickly to mind is the location of Point Hope, directly in the path of the annual northward migration of the bowhead whale. However, archeological evidence tells us that Ipiutak people did no whaling but lived on walrus, hair seal, and the huge 900-pound *ugrug*, or bearded seal.

If they did no whaling, their direct descendants do. Indeed, their lives center around the pursuit of the world's mightiest living mammal. "Leads" are the narrow channels of open water between ice floes. They form close to the land at Point Hope, making both whale and seal hunting relatively easy in winter and spring. The villagers are among the best ice hunters in Alaska. In

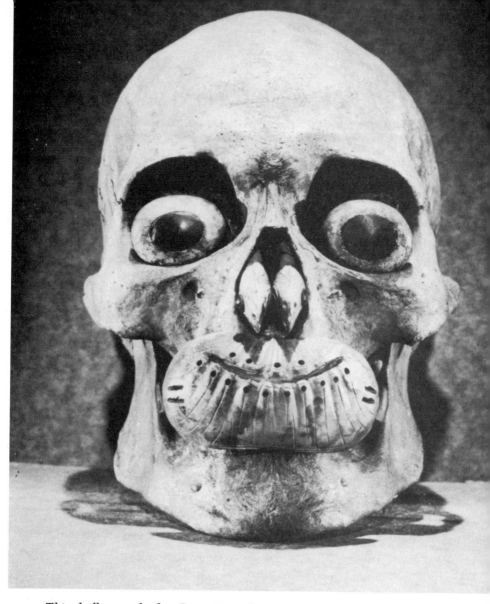

This skull unearthed at Point Hope has ivory eyes inlaid with pupils of jet, and an ivory nose plug and mouth cover.

summer when the ice is gone and land game is scarce the men, like so many other village Eskimos, move to larger villages or to Fairbanks looking for jobs that will bring cash money into the family.

In 1935, back in the days just after the Great Depression, when Alaska was still a territory, 200 families from the relief rolls of several northern states were transported to the Matanuska Valley of Alaska near Palmer to begin a new life. With the help of the federal government, transport was provided, and money loaned for equipment, land purchase, buildings, livestock, and even furniture. By the fall of the next year the farmers' newly built barns were bulging with harvested crops, and the new town of Palmer was flourishing. The experiment known as the Matanuska Colony was born in controversy but managed to grow and thrive. With Alaska's increasing population came an increased demand for fresh milk, cream, and vegetables. Combined with Palmer's excellent road, rail, and air connections a prosperous future for the colony seemed assured.

There were 12 farms in Alaska at the beginning of the twentieth century. Their number gradually increased to 639 by 1939, but thereafter improved technology and cheaper, speedier air transportation allowed imported food to compete successfully with locally grown products, and the number of farms declined to 310. The Matanuska Valley around Palmer is still the most important farm area in Alaska, growing 70 percent of the total output. The Tanana Valley, Kenai Peninsula, Southwest, and Southeast compete in that order. But only 5 percent of the food eaten in Alaska is grown there. Like almost everything else in the state, farming is more expensive than in the lower 48. The climate is difficult, the season is short, the cost of labor is high. On the plus side, many insects that plague farmers in warmer climates are absent, and the remaining farms are now larger and more productive than formerly. The long summer days limit fiber formation in some vegetables, producing better quality carrots, beets, cabbage, broccoli, and turnips. It is in freezing and exporting these high-quality vegetables that Alaska's successful farming future may lie.

Only a small number of people are engaged in year-round farming in Alaska. The 80 dairies that were operating in 1960 followed the farming pattern and were reduced ten years later to 35. The small marginal operation can no longer compete successfully with the larger well-capitalized farm.

As Fairbanks is the market for most of the Tanana Valley farming, so Anchorage, 50 miles away, is Palmer's chief consumer. Palmer's setting between two dramatic glacier-studded mountain ranges, the Talkeetnas and the Chugachs, makes it a delightful goal for pleasure trips. Sunflowers reaching to the second story of a house and sweet peas ten feet tall with enormous blossoms are common in Palmer and throughout southeastern and south central Alaska. Every familiar flower seems taller, bigger, and brighter than those we are accustomed to in more southerly latitudes.

Ketchikan, the southernmost good-sized city in Alaska, has been described as three blocks wide and three miles long. One approaches it by ship through islands of green forest, gliding along mirror-still waters. It is a major port of entry and a growing industrial center.

Strung out thinly along a narrow strip of land at the foot of sharply rising Deer Mountain, Ketchikan seems in imminent danger of tumbling into the waters of Tongass Narrows. Every square inch of the crowded city has been utilized, and when new streets are needed it is said that they must be blasted out of the solid rock.

A giant pulp mill, one of the largest in the world, is in Ketchikan. It is a relatively new year-round industry for Alaska and employs many people. Timber for the mill is cut from the Tongass National Forest's 16 million acres of virgin timber, which occupy most of southeastern Alaska. All cutting is under the strict supervision of the U.S. Forest Service. Alaska's other large pulp mill is at Sitka.

Ketchikan has skyscraper apartment buildings, modern schools, and attractive new housing developments. The 11,400 people who live there enjoy the cool summers, which resemble those of the Maine coast. There is little snowfall in winter, but in all seasons there is rain, rain, and more rain. The abundant rainfall is responsible for ideal tree growing conditions in the area and also for the famous Ketchikan flower gardens. Delphiniums reach eight or nine feet, pansies grow as big as saucers. Although no road connects Ketchikan with other towns, the streets are crowded with automobiles. The city is in touch with the rest of Alaska and "outside" through shipping, the Alaska Marine Highway system, and numerous daily flights. A new multimillion dollar airport was completed in 1973.

Alaska's Farthest North

A glance at a polar projection map of the northern hemisphere, or better, at the top of a globe, shows the countries of the North grouped around a smallish sea called the Arctic Ocean; more accurately, it is a Polar Mediterranean. As the Old World Mediterranean lies between Europe and Africa, so the northernmost body of water, surrounded by the powerful nations of the world, lies between North America with Greenland, Canada, and Alaska on one side, and northern Europe and Asia on the other.

On the shores of the Polar Mediterranean the most northerly cape in our most northerly state is Point Barrow. As the planes fly it is 500 miles northeast of Nome and the same distance northwest of Fairbanks. Its Eskimo name is Nuwuk, meaning "the point." Our name for it dates from 1826 when Captain Beechey named it after Sir John Barrow, the great British patron of Arctic exploration who was responsible for his Parliament's offering a 20,000-pound reward to the first navigator of the Northwest Passage.

About nine miles southwest of Point Barrow is the village of Barrow. It was here that a trading post was first established in 1885 by the later-famous Charles D. Brower. Charlie Brower played host to many famous explorers in the more than 50 years he lived in Barrow. Humorist Will Rogers and pilot Wiley Post were on their way to visit him when their plane crashed and they lost their lives. In his book, *Fifty Years Below Zero*, Brower gives the highlights of his long and interesting life. Tom Brower, Charles's son, continued the family tradition as an unofficial greeter and influential citizen.

Nowadays a great many more people turn up at Barrow than ever did in Charlie Brower's day. Barrow's population (2,207 in 1980) has doubled since 1950, and it now has the largest Eskimo

Ketchikan is strung out along a narrow strip of land at the foot of Deer Mountain. Note the fishing boats in the harbor.

settlement in the United States. Its growth is mainly due to the employment opportunities offered by a constellation of federal government departments, the Bureau of Indian Affairs office, the U.S. Public Health Service's 14-bed hospital, and the Office of Naval Research's Arctic Research Laboratory (NARL).

NARL, established in 1947 in a quonset hut of the Naval Petroleum Reserve No. 4 not far from Barrow, was the only U.S. scientific station devoted entirely to Arctic basic research. When the navy finished its oil exploration in the area, the lab inherited the quonset hut village left behind. It grew to have a permanent staff of about 100. There were always another 100 visiting scientists and researchers from universities and other government departments who came for long or short periods depending on the type of investigation they were pursuing. Owned by the navy, it was run by contract with the University of Alaska through a

An aerial view of NARL in 1968.

Wolves, along with many other Arctic animals, were maintained in the NARL zoo for scientific study.

civilian administrator. Its research projects covered a geographical area stretching from Bering Strait to Greenland and including the Polar Sea. It had its own fleet of half a dozen specially equipped aircraft, tracked vessels, motor-driven sleds, and other vehicles needed to support researchers working inland, along the coast, out on the sea ice, or in the air. It had its own research library, museum, and private zoo whose tenants varied from year to year but usually included polar bears, wolves, wolverines, snowy owls, and other animals interesting to biologists and physiologists. In addition to the quonset hut village, NARL had a remarkable permanent building completed in 1968 which was probably the most modern architectural complex in our Far North. To prevent the heat of the buildings from thawing the permafrost below, the building was mounted on 557 piles sunk 15 feet into the frozen ground with an air space left between ground and building. Its seven wings housed 41 separate modern laboratories for performing every imaginable kind of research, as well as attractive living quarters and common rooms for staff and visitors, painted in many different colors.

It was from this center of Arctic learning that the famous ice island floating scientific stations in the Polar Sea were staffed and supported. Drifting laboratories like T-3 (Fletcher's Ice Island) and ARLIS II (Arctic Research Laboratory Ice Station No. 2) are a wonderful means of obtaining scientific information about what is happening above, below, and in the sea ice in areas where ships cannot operate without the gravest danger, if at all, because of the ice.

The lab even had an important role in the local whaling operations, which continue to be an important food source for the local Eskimos, as well as those at Point Hope, Wainwright, and Gambell. It was from radio monitors placed by NARL that the first warning of an approaching whale came.

Long- and short-term scientific programs in oceanography,

Max Brewer, the first director of NARL, with two young Arctic wolverines, ages five weeks (foreground) and nine weeks.

geology, geophysics, sea ice, permafrost, underwater acoustics, northern biology, adaptations of man and animals to cold, and many other areas were conducted from the lab. Despite the difficult climate, the absence of roads, problems of permafrost, and flights cancelled because of weather, the NARL was a cheerful, busy place. Scientists, technicians, and secretaries in an atmosphere of cheery purposefulness were all "doing their thing" and providing the rest of us with the knowledge we needed to operate at greater efficiency in the Far North while safeguarding the ecological balance.

All that changed when the navy shifted its research base to Greenland in 1977. The federal government has since been pondering the fate of the laboratory, which is now virtually unused. Although many groups have tried to get another federal agency to oversee the facility, it was closed in late 1982. Alaska's junior senator, Frank Murkowski, stated prior to its closing, "The closure of the laboratory would leave a void that the nation's scientific community would be hard pressed to fill."

An innovation of recent years at Barrow is the tourist business. In summer extra flights bring vacationers from many parts of the continent—people who want to set foot on the northernmost tip of Alaska, see how the Eskimos live, and perhaps have a ride in a skin-covered umiak. Barrow Eskimos, although most of them receive high wages working six days a week for the government, still hunt walrus and whale as their ancestors did. The Top of the World Hotel at Point Barrow, owned and operated by Eskimos, accommodates visitors. If the weather is nippy, and it usually is here even in summer, fur-trimmed parkas are supplied by the airline hostesses.

Further tourist entertainment is provided of a summer evening at the Eskimo Dance House. Here to the accompaniment of high-pitched singing and the hypnotic sound of a dozen drums beating complicated rhythms in perfect unison, Eskimo dances are performed in full costume. While tourists make up the larger part of the audience, they are joined by middle-aged and older local

Drum dance at Barrow. Eskimos formerly had no word of greeting. Now koyanak, *which means "excellent," is used in many areas.*

residents who love to hear the old songs and see the traditional dances. The younger set seems to prefer more modern dancing down the street a bit, to the strains of the juke box. At a distance they look like any group of teen-agers in more southerly places.

Barrow is in truly Arctic country. More than 300 miles north of the Arctic Circle, it is far from any warm currents like those of the Gulf Stream that bathe the northern coasts of Norway in similar latitudes. Here great masses of ice, pressed forward by wind and current, grind against the shore in winter, producing the heaviest ice pack known in any part of the world. There is permafrost here; only from about 6 to 18 inches of the earth's surface thaws downward in summer. Because of the permafrost below, the hot sun above, and the absence of sidewalks, the streets are muddy, and boots, whether rubber or sealskin, are a must. The frost below the surface, which creates so many building problems, happily provides free refrigeration for food storage chambers dug into frozen soil. Meat has been kept fresh for years in these natural deepfreezes. Where the vegetation is undisturbed, the meadows are covered with rich grass.

As in all other towns in the permafrost zone of Alaska, water for drinking, cooking, and bathing presents a problem. In Point Barrow and similar towns, water must be hauled, often from great distances, and is sold by the drum, making bathing an expensive luxury. Water for laundry and cleaning purposes must also be purchased, increasing the already fearfully high cost of living. But if the cost of living is high, so are wages.

A worldwide problem that has accompanied the population explosion is the disposal of human wastes, trash, garbage, and sewage. In a place like Barrow the problem is compounded because permafrost prevents any underground sewage disposal, and cold above ground makes natural decay incredibly slow. Early explorers used to report with surprise finding tracks of vehicles, wood chips, and campfire remnants that looked as though they had just been made, but had actually been made a century before. For thousands of years the Eskimos occupied the surrounding areas leaving so few traces of their passage that it takes a trained archeologist to detect their camping places. Modern man with his oversupply of plastic, paper, and metal containers and his inability to think of others has left scenes of the most horrible disorder all over the Arctic (as well as in lower latitudes).

The Eskimos, who have picked up many of our bad habits, have recently acquired one more. Living as we do in one place, buying our kind of canned and packaged foods in the local store, they too now have ugly little dump heaps outside the back of their houses.

It is ironic that Barrow had closed-circuit TV and a relatively rich cash economy some years before it had its own high school. Until the late 1970s Barrow Eskimos had to leave home if they wanted to continue their education after grade school. The new

The U.S.S. Nautilus *welcomed home to Groton, Connecticut. PANOPOS (on signs) stands for "Pacific Atlantic North Pole."*

high school contains a kitchen, gym, and—a genuine innovation for Barrow youngsters—a swimming pool! Oil revenues enable this school system, as well as others in Alaska, to be free of worries about funds during yearly budget meetings. In fact, money is so prevalent that often local high school sports teams—and sometimes fans—are flown to the lower 48 at great expense to compete against other teams.

The tip of our northernmost sandspit is not the boundary marking the end of all activity. Yankee whalers learned a century ago that fortunes could be built in Massachusetts on whalebone from the sea beyond the coast. Stefansson proved on his 1913–18 sledge journeys over the ice that life in the sea does not cease beyond where ships are able to penetrate. His party lived by hunting seals as they traveled afoot over the moving pack ice many hundreds of miles north of Alaskan land. Later Ivan Papanin and his colleagues demonstrated, in 1937, that the waters of the Polar Mediterranean are teeming with animal and plant life even at the very North Pole, more than 1,000 miles north of Barrow. Recently there have been many scientific stations set down on ice islands in the polar pack, both by the Soviets and by us.

In August of 1958 the nuclear-powered submarine *Nautilus* completed a passage under the pack ice, from Bering Strait to the North Pole, emerging in the Greenland Sea north of Iceland. Her sister ship, the *Skate*, soon afterward made the same magnificent journey in the opposite direction, surfacing through the ice at the North Pole. Three hundred miles to the south, on the Alaska side, they surfaced again to greet and visit with the scientists on the drifting ice station *Alpha*, engaged in International Geophysical Year investigations.

In the Arctic, the North Pole is the center of a deep, liquid sea. This is exactly opposite to the Antarctic, where the South Pole is the center of a huge ice-covered continent. A surprising number of people still hold the erroneous belief, which dates back to classic Greek times, that the Arctic Sea is frozen to the bottom. Another misconception was encouraged by almost every newspaper and magazine reporting the *Nautilus* voyage, stating that the submarine traveled below the "icecap under the North Pole." There is no icecap at, under, or anywhere near the North Pole. By definition, an icecap is a large, land-based glacier composed of fresh ice, which in earlier times was newly fallen snow. The relatively thin, fractured shell of ice that floats on our northernmost sea is salt water ice, which has a different composition, freezing point, color, texture, and behavior under pressure or melting than fresh ice. Sea ice may range in thickness from fractions of an inch to a maximum thickness of 11 to 13 feet.

Arctic Sea ice would resemble a thin, smooth shell, were it not for winds and currents. Winds, however gentle, and currents, however sluggish, are sufficient to break the cover into ice floes of every imaginable shape and size and to keep them constantly on the move. In winter they move rather slowly; in summer they move somewhat more freely, the spaces between floes widening to reveal more patches of blue, open water. In midsummer as much as 25 percent of the Polar Sea may be open water where whales and submarines alike may surface with ease.

Winds and currents that break the ice cover are also responsible for grinding the floes against each other at their edges or for piling them up into pressure ridges against the landfast shore ice, where it meets the moving pack. These pressure ridges, startling and dramatic in size and shape, are seldom higher above water than 100 feet. Two hundred feet therefore is about the maximum thickness of sea ice above and below water. A pressure ridge is usually pyramid-shaped, the base of the pyramid below water level.

Another misconception about the Arctic Sea is that it is filled with innumerable icebergs. Practically speaking, there are no icebergs in the Arctic Sea. Greenland, our greatest northern iceberg factory, discharges its bergs to the east and west, but all are borne southward by the prevailing currents, and eventually they die in the warm waters of the North Atlantic. All icebergs were once part of a glacier and their ice is therefore fresh. When a glacier extends down to the sea and out over the water, it is the floating section that breaks off to become an iceberg, and the birth process is called *calving*.

To further complicate the differences between salt and fresh ice, salt sea ice when it is sufficiently old, becomes fresh. In alternate freezing and thawing that occurs with the changing season, the salt content of sea ice migrates toward whichever side is warmer, usually downward, and the briny particles are eventually eliminated. When sea ice is more than two years old its melt water can be used for drinking. After three years, no saltiness in floating sea ice can be detected except by delicate chemical test—the human palate cannot taste it. This has been known for centuries by the practical sealers and whalers who wintered often in the North.

Thanks to the drifting ice stations we now know the path of the Arctic Ocean currents. Oceanographers have charted the mountains and valleys of the undersea landscape and can tell their age and origin. Marine biologists have described the live inhabitants of the cold, salty water and the astonishing activity of tiny creatures on the underside of the pack ice. Physicists explain the

The shore lead off Point Barrow where the migrating whales pass. Two whaling camps are visible on the horizon.

crystalline structure of the sea ice. Zoologists have studied and listed the animals that walk on and fly over the ice. Still others measure and record aspects of the climate as far as rockets will go. On the land similar investigations have wiped out innumerable blank spots in our knowledge.

Our little world has been entirely discovered and we must close the book of primary exploration and open two others. The first is that of outer space and the universe as a whole. The second is the exploration of ways and means of preserving and improving our decaying, polluted, overpopulated spaceship earth.

Just as we now know how to build on permafrost without deforming the land and how to travel in the Arctic without destroying the fragile ecosystem, the knowledge of how to preserve our planet has accumulated. The looming question of paramount importance is—will we use it?

INDEX

Admiralty Island, 123
Affirmative action program, 13
Agattu Island, 142
Agnew, Spiro, 13
Airplane (see Transportation: airplane)
Akutan Island, 139
Alaska Bilingual Education Bill, 70
Alaska Department of Fish and Game, 124
Alaska Eskimo Whaling Commission (AEWC), 99-100
Alaska Federation of Natives (AFN), 30
Alaska Festival of Native Arts, 146
Alaska Highway, 78, 93, 149
Alaska Hospital, 147
Alaska Integrated Communications Enterprise (see White Alice)
Alaska Juneau Mine, 108
Alaska Marine Highway System, 80, 109, 131, 159
Alaska Native Brotherhood, 39
Alaska Native Claims Settlement Act, 11, 27-29, 146
Alaska Native Language Center, 68, 70-71
Alaska Native Service Hospital, 43, 147
Alaska Natural Gas Transportation System (ANGTS), 15, 16
Alaska Purchase, 21, 101, 104, 121

Alaska Railroad, 77, 143, 149
Alaska Range, 3, 132, 143
Alaska Road Commission, 78
Alaska's Native People, 31
Alaska State Council on the Arts, 38
Alaska State Ferry System, 29
Alaska Statehood Act, 21
Aleutian Islands, 25, 68, 120, 123, 124, 132-142
Aleuts, 31-32, 123, 133-134
  lands of, 21, 27-28
  language of, 137
  population, 25
Alexander Archipelago, 80
Alpha (drifting ice station), 169
Alyeska Pipeline Service, 2, 3, 8, 10, 13-14
Amchitka Island, 136
American Association of Indian Affairs, 30
American Museum of Natural History, 152
Anchorage, 2, 15, 21, 27, 30, 76, 106, 111, 112, 119, 143-147, 151, 157
Anchorage Daily News, 143
Anchorage Historical and Fine Arts Museum, 146
Anchorage Times, 112
Anderson, Charles, 146
Andreanof Islands, 132, 139, 141
Angoon, 80
Anthropology studies, 153

173

Archeological finds, 152–153
Archeological sites, 14
Arctic Circle, 72, 74, 94, 132, 155, 166
Arctic Manual, 47
Arctic National Wildlife Range, 8
Arctic Ocean (Polar Mediterranean), 159, 168, 170
Arctic Research Laboratory Ice Station (ARLIS II), 164
Arctic Sea, 21, 50, 80, 81
Arctic Slope, 3
Athabascan Indians, 32
Athabascan language, 68
Atka Island, 32, 133, 137, 138, 139–140
Attu Island, 137, 138, 142
Atwood, Robert, 111–112
Auk Lake, 111
Aurora borealis, 152
Aviation (*see* Transportation: airplane)

Barabaras, 31, 32
Baranof, Alexander, 101–102, 131
Baranof Hotel, 109
Barrow, 42, 159, 162, 165, 166, 167, 168
Barrow, Sir John, 159
Bartlett, E. L., 20, 21, 31
Basket weaving, 32, 139–140
Beechey, Captain, 159
Bering, Vitus, 116, 136
Bering Island, 136
Bering Sea, 21, 50, 121, 123, 132, 133, 139
Bering Strait, 21, 95, 163, 169
Big Diomede Island, 115
Bird life, 121
Blanket weaving, 37
Bockstoce, John, 98
Brady, John, 107
Brink, Frank, 131
Bristol Bay, 133
Brooks Range, 3, 74
Brower, Charles D., 42, 159
Brower, Tom, 159
Bureau of Indian Affairs, 28, 29, 70, 106, 127, 162
Bush pilot, 77, 125

Canol (Canadian Oil) project, 16–17
Capital Site Planning Commission, 113
Capital Site Selection Committee, 112
Carter, Jimmy, 16
Central Fox Islands, 139
Chena River, 149
Chilkat Indians, 37
Chugach Mountains, 3, 143, 158
Climate, 10, 72–75, 83, 89, 90, 132, 149–150
Communications, 83, 85, 88–89, 143, 147 (*see also* White Alice)
Comsat, 147
Convention on Conservation of North Pacific Fur Seals, 122
Cook Inlet, 144
Cook Inlet-Kenai Peninsula, 2, 15
Cordova, 80
Crafts, 32, 37, 39, 128–129, 139–140, 146, 155
Craig, 80
"Cry of the Wild Ram," 131

Deer Mountain, 158
Denali National Monument, 78
Denali National Park, 78
Depression, 156
De Stoeckl, Baron, 101
DEW (Distant Early Warning) line, 21, 81, 85, 147
Dickey, Don, 23
Diomede Islands, 115–116, 118–119
Dog sled, 54, 56–58
Douglas, 108
Dutch Harbor, 137, 139, 141

Earthquake, 146
Education, 27, 29, 69–70, 151–152, 167
Egan, William A., 20
Elmendorf Field, 147
"Energy crisis," 12
Environmental Defense Fund, 7
Epidemics, 42–43
Eskimo, 134, 159
    children, 61–64
    clothing, 58, 60–61

customs, 66–67
lands, 21, 27–28, 32
language, 64–66, 67–68
population, 25
Eskimo, Indian, Aleut Publishing Company, 31
Eskimo-Aleut language, 68–69, 70
Eskimo Dance House, 165
Eskimos, 39–50, 134, 145, 153, 159, 164, 165, 167–168
children, 61–64
clothing, 58, 60–61
customs, 66–67
fuel use, 41, 118
housing, 27, 46–50
lands, 21, 27–28, 32
language, 64–66, 67–68
population, 25
whaling, 98–99
Exploration, early, 116

Fairbanks, 3, 11, 21, 41, 74, 76, 77, 80, 106, 112, 148–151, 157, 159
Farming, 95, 157
Fifty Years Below Zero, 159
Fishing, 21, 23, 29, 40, 90, 92, 109, 134, 143
Fletcher's Ice Island (T-3), 164
Flowers, 158
Folklore, 152
Forestry industry, 92–93
Fort Richardson, 147
Fortune, 37
Fort Yukon, 74
Fossils, 152
Fox Islands, 132, 134, 139
Friends of Animals, 122
Friends of the Earth, 7
Fur industry, 95
Fur Seal Act, 31

Gambell, 164
Gas pipeline, 15
Gas (*see* Natural gas)
Gastineau Channel, 107
Gates of the Arctic National Park, 78
"Gee pole," 58
Geist, Dr. Otto W., 152

Geophysical Institute, 150, 152
Giddings, Louis, 153
Glaciers, 152
Gold, 1, 94–95, 107, 108, 139, 148
Gravel, Mike, 13
Great Circle Polar Routes, 76, 81, 144–145
Greek Orthodox Church, 136–137
Gruening, Ernest, 20, 90
Gulf of Alaska, 2, 130

Haida Indians, 32, 34
Haines, 80
Hammond, Jay, 18, 113
Harris, 107
Harris, Frank, 112
Health problems, 42–43, 45–46
Herman, Father, 131
Hershel Island, 95, 96
Hickel, Walter, 5, 16
"Hickel Highway," 3–4
Hollis, 80
Homer, 80
Hoonah, 80
Housing, 1, 27, 46–50, 143
Hovercraft, 87
Humane Society, 122
Hunting, 32, 34, 40–41, 50, 118, 119, 121–122, 134, 136

Iceberg, 170
Icecap, 169
Ice fog, 149–150
Ice island floating scientific stations, 164
Igloos, 46–50
Iliuliuk Bay, 139
Income, per capita, 25
Indian NaDene language, 68
Indian River Park, 107
Indians, 32, 34, 37, 43, 68, 69, 102, 104, 153
lands of, 21, 27–28
languages of, 68–70
population, 25
Ingalik, 32
International Date Line, 115, 142

International Whaling Commission (IWC), 99–100
Inupiat Paitot (People's Heritage), 30
Ipiutak, 155
Isanotski Strait (False Pass), 138
Islands of the Four Mountains, 132
Ivory carvings, 155

Jackson, Sheldon, 106
Japonski Island, 105
Juneau, 80, 107–111, 112, 151
Juneau Museum, 37

Kake, 80
Katalla, 2
Katmai National Park, 78
Kayak, 50–52, 54, 129, 136
Kenai Peninsula, 2, 16, 146, 157
Ketchikan, 37, 80, 93, 158
Kiska Island, 137
Klawock, 80
Klondike gold rush, 139
Kodiak, 80
Kodiak Historical Society and Museum, 126
Kodiak Island, 101, 130–131
Korovin Volcano, 139
Krauss, Michael, 68, 70–71
Kiska, 141

Languages, 64–66, 67–69, 70, 137, 152
Larsen, Helge, 153
Legislature, 107
Little Diomede Island, 115, 118
Lumber industry, 23, 158

Mackenzie River, 6
Mackenzie Valley, 7
Mukushin Volcano, 139
Mammoths, 153
Manhattan, 6
Matanuska Colony, 157
Matanuska Valley, 95, 156–157
Measles, 42
Mekoryuk, 129
Mendenhall Glacier, 109
Metlakatla, 80
Military installations, 147

Missionaries, 68, 69, 126, 136
Morgan, Lael, 31
Morton, Rogers C. B., 5, 8, 12, 13
Mosquitoes, 74
Mount Edgecumbe, 103, 105
Mount Edgecumbe Boarding School, 106
Mount Juneau, 107
Mount McKinley, 23–25, 78, 113
Mount McKinley National Park, 77–78
Mount Roberts, 107
Murkowski, Frank, 165
Museums, 106, 126, 146
Muskeg, 152
Musk-ox, 124, 151
Musk-Ox Project, 125–126

Nakasone, Yasuhiro, 16
NASA Satellite ATS-1, 90
National Center for Biomedical Communications, 90
National Environmental Protection Agency (NEPA), 13
National Environment Policy Act, 5
Native Arts and Crafts Center, 146
Native Arts and Craft Service, 130
Native Claims Settlement Act, 37, 70
Native crafts, 139–140
Native history, 152
Native languages, 152
Native population:
   changes in, 29–32
   and culture shock, 26–27
   early treatment of, 26
   (*see also* Aleuts; Eskimos; Indians)
Natural gas, 2, 8, 15, 25, 90
Nautilus, 169
Naval Arctic Research Laboratory (NARL), 162–165
Naval Petroleum Reserve No. 4, 162
Near Islands, 132, 142
New Archangel, 102
New York Times, 6
Nikolski, 134
Nixon, Richard M., 5, 11, 13, 27
Nome, 119, 159
Northern Agricultural Research, 125
North Pole, 169

North Slope, 1, 2, 6, 7, 8, 15, 16, 114, 149
Nunivak Island, 123, 124, 125, 126–130

Oil, 1, 2, 4, 8, 13–14, 23, 25, 90, 95, 143,
    146–147, 162
Otter Island, 119

Palmer, 157
Papanin, Ivan, 168
Parks, 78
Pedro, Felix, 148
Pelican, 80
Permafrost, 3, 8–10, 74, 86, 148, 152,
    153, 166, 172
    zones of, 8
Permanent Fund, 18
Petersburg, 80
Petroleum industry (*see* Oil)
Pioneers Home, 106
Pogromni Volcano, 139
Point Barrow, 6, 8, 19, 72, 77, 98, 124,
    147, 159, 165
Point Hope (Tigerak), 98, 153, 155, 164
Polar Mediterranean (*see* Arctic
    Ocean)
Polar Sea, 6
Polar Sea, 81, 151, 153, 155, 163,
    169–170
Population, state, 25
Port Lions, 80
Post, Wiley, 159
Potlatch, 34, 37
Pressure ridges, 170
Pribilof, Gavriil, 119–120
Pribilof Islands (Seal), 31, 95, 119–123,
    134
Pribilof seal, 120, 121
Prince William Sound, 2
Prospect Creek, 74
Providence Hospital, 147
Prudhoe Bay, 1, 2, 6, 8, 14, 16, 18, 25
Prudhoe Bay–Valdez pipeline, 74
Pulp industry, 23

Radio communications, 83
    short-wave, 88–89
Railroads, 77

Rainey, Froelich G., 153
Rat Islands, 132, 136, 141
RCA Alascom, 85
Reed, Irene, 71
Reindeer, 126–128
Rivers, Ralph J., 20
Rock, Howard, 30–31
Rogers, George, 27
Rogers, Will, 159
Rolligon, 87
Russia, 31 (*see also* Soviet Union)
Russian America, 68–70, 134, 136
Russian America Company, 40, 134
Russian Orthodox Church, 68, 105,
    131, 139

Saint George Island, 119, 120, 123
St. Lawrence Island, 98
Saint Michael's Cathedral, 105
Saint Paul Island, 31, 119, 120, 121, 123
Salmon industry, 92
Saxman Park, 37
Sea ice, 169
Sealaska Corporation, 37–38
Sealion Rock, 119
Seal Islands (*see* Pribilof Islands)
Seals, 119, 120, 121–123, 155
Sea otters, 134, 136
Seaton, Fred, 20
Seldovia, 80
Sewage (*see* Waste disposal)
Seward, 77, 80
Seward, William Henry, 101
Seward Peninsula, 124
Sheffield, Bill, 18
Sheldon Jackson School, 105–106
Shellfish industry, 92
Shishaldin Volcano (Smoking Moses),
    139
Shrimp, 92
Sitka, 80, 101–107, 131, 158
Sitka National Monument Park, 37,
    107
Size, state, 25
Skagway, 80
Skate, 169
Sled dogs, 54, 56–58

Solovief, 139
Southeastern System, 80
Soviet Union, 21, 142 (*see also* Russia)
S .S. *Arco Juneau*, 14
Statehood, 19–21
State income tax, 1
State Museum, 39
State of Alaska, 20
Stefansson, Vilhjalmur, xi, 168
Stepovich, Mike, 20

Taiga, 32
Talkeetna, 147
Talkeetna Mountains, 158
Tanana River, 149
Tanana Valley, 95, 149, 157
TAPS (Trans Alaska Pipeline System), 2
Teal, John, 125
Tenakee Springs, 80
Tennessee Plan, 19
Territorial Legislature, 19
Thorne Bay, 80
Tigerak (*see* Point Hope)
Timber industry, 158
Tlingit-Haida Council, 39
Tlingit Indians, 32, 34, 37, 68, 69, 102, 104
Tongass Narrows, 158
Tongass National Forest, 158
Tonsina River, 14
Top of the World Hotel, 165
Totem poles, 37, 107
Tourism, 23, 25, 93–94, 165
Trans Alaska Pipeline (*see* TAPS)
Trans Alaska Pipeline Authorization Act, 13
Transportation, 85
  airplane, 75–77, 81, 143
  ferry system, 80
  railroad, 77, 143, 149
Tuberculosis, 42, 43
Tundra Times, 30, 31

Umiak, 54, 98, 118, 119, 129, 165
Umnak Island, 134
Unalaska, 31, 137, 139
Unalaska Bay, 139
Unimak Island, 138
U.S. Army Corps of Engineers, 16
U.S. Coast Guard, 119
U.S. Forest Service, 158
U.S. Public Health Service, 42
U.S. Public Health Service Hospital, 162
U.S. Smelting, Refining and Mining Company, 148, 152
University of Alaska, 19, 27, 70, 90, 109, 125, 151, 162
  Geophysical Institute, 150, 152
  museum, 152

Valdez, 2, 11, 14, 18, 20, 80
Veniaminov, Ivan, 68, 136
Volcanoes, 132, 139

Wainwright, 98, 164
Walrus, 155
Walrus Island, 119
Waste disposal, 167
Water problems, 167
Weather reports, 90
Whaling, 95–100, 139, 155, 164, 168
White Alice (communications system), 21, 83, 147
White Pass and Yukon Railroad, 77
Whittier, 80
Wilderness Society, 7
"Williwaw," 132
Willow, 112–114
World War II, 137, 141
Wrangell, 80
Wrangell-Saint Elias National Park, 78

Yukon Territory, 77
Yukon River, 13, 72, 149
Yukon Valley, 74